FINDING DOLLARS FOR FAMILY FUN

Also by Gwen Weising

Raising Kids on Purpose for the Fun of It
Finding Time for Family Fun

FINDING DOLLARS FOR FAMILY FUN

Creating Happy Memories on a Budget

GWEN WEISING

Fleming H. Revell
A Division of Baker Book House
Grand Rapids, Michigan 49516

This book is dedicated to God,
who has given us enough to take care of us
but not so much
as to take away our dependence on him—
the Source of all things

CONTENTS

Introduction   9

1. Money: A Tool for Family Fun   11

A Money-Attitude Checkup • Start Simply • Balancing Spending and Saving • Budgets Are Back • Why Spend Money on Fun? • Family Adventures for Little or No Money

2. How Do We Get the Money We Need?   23

A Quick History of Work • One Income versus Two • What Does It Cost for a Mother to Work? •Kids Can Work, Too • Is Part-time Work Best? • Is Working at Home the Answer? • Family Adventures for Little or No Money

3. Teach Your Children about Money   39

Talk about Money • Teach Your Children about Budgets • Teach Your Child about the Family Budget • Teach Them to Give to God • Teach Them to Give to Others • Teach Them to Care for What You Have • Teach Them to Use and Reuse What You Have • Teach Them to Enjoy Possessions as Investments • People Are More Important Than Things • Family Adventures for Little or No Money

4. Su Casa, Mi Casa   53

What Do We Need? • How Can We Know What We Need? • What Do We Want? • Can We Afford What We Want? • Other Kinds of Housing • How to Buy a House • Family Adventures for Little or No Money

5. Put Another Potato in the Soup   67

Making Food Dollars Stretch • Some Factors That Affect How Much You Spend • Free Food • Food Warehouses • Growing Your

Own • Putting By • When It Comes to Entertaining • Ideas for Saving Food Dollars • Family Adventures for Little or No Money

6. *Vogue, GQ,* **and Other Expensive Myths** 87

Buy Quality • Sewing to Have More Clothes • Mending to Have More Clothes • Restyling: Not as Hard as You Think • Accessorizing for Maximum Mileage • Outlet Shopping • Thrifting • Resale Shops • Garage Sales • Swapping • Shopping in Your Closet • What's on Sale This Month? • Family Adventures for Little or No Money

7. **The Decorating Shoestring** 111

Furnishings Set the Tone • What to Look for When Choosing Furniture • Where to Find Furniture • How Can I Know Excellent Quality? • What about Floor Coverings? • What about Appliances? • Accessories • Ideas for Saving Money on Home Decorating • Family Adventures for Little or No Money

8. **Wheels** 135

Do You Need a Car? • How Many Cars Do You Need? • Buying the First Family Car • How Long Should You Keep the Car? • What Kind of Interior Is Best? • How to Shop for a Car • Getting the Money to Buy a Car • Alternate Forms of Transportation • Family Adventures for Little or No Money

9. **Traveling When You Can't Afford It** 147

Where to Go • Set Goals for Family Travel • Where Will You Sleep? • Let's Go Camping • Packing for a Trip • Money-Saving Ideas for Travel • Camping Equipment • Family Adventures for Little or No Money

10. **Get It Free** 165

Free Musical Events • Free Theater • Swapping • What Are the Neighbors Throwing Out? • Free Animals • The Public Library • Free Sporting Events • Your Turn • Family Adventures for Little or No Money

11. **Get It Cheap** 175

Salvage Shops • Swap Meets • Garage Sales • Auctions and Everything Else • Conclusion • Family Adventures for Little or No Money

Endnotes 183
Bibliography 185

₁INTRODUCTION

₁ remember the first time I ever worked for money, picking potatoes in Montana. We showed up at the field early one fall morning. The air was crisp, and as I knelt on the ground, the damp soil left muddy patches on the knees of my blue jeans. By midday the sun was pouring its heat onto our bent backs and the dirt had turned to warm brown powder.

I remember the noisy potato digger as it passed up and down the rows, bringing up and laying bare to the autumn air the hidden treasure of the earth. There the potatoes lay, naked and exposed, waiting for us to pick them up and drop them, one at a time, into our wire buckets.

I can still feel the cutting edge of the bucket against the inside of my knees as I steadied it and tipped its contents into a potato sack. Those brown burlap bags stood at attention behind us like a row of soldiers, guarding our day's pay.

Soon a big flatbed truck passed through the fields and took our sacks away to the potato cellar, to be stored there until the price for potatoes reached its zenith. At the end of the day we picked up our pay. I think we made about twenty cents a bag.

I don't remember what I bought with my money, but I do remember that Mom bought a set of English pottery dishes. She still has them, and now they've become somewhat valuable, since the company no longer makes that kind of dish.

9

Potato picking is hard, backbreaking work. I've done a lot of things since then to earn money, but I don't think I ever worked harder than I did that day. But work is work, and wages are the congealed sweat of our efforts. Since money is so hard to come by, we need to think of every possible way to stretch our dollars.

The purpose of this book is to teach us how to earn and use money in such a way that we don't sacrifice our families on the altar of employment. Too many families in this country are being sacrificed because both parents are working—and working—and working, to provide *things* for their children. If the truth were known, our children would probably rather have our time and attention than the things our wages buy them. Nothing can take a parent's place in a child's life. In this book, I will tell you how to make a little money go a long way, so you don't have to work all the time and still will have some money left for doing fun things with your children.

I'm not talking about investing, financial planning, or long-term savings plans. There are lots of books on those subjects. I'm going to tell you how to save money on everyday things and find inexpensive (or free) ways to have fun as a family.

Doing this doesn't involve lowering your quality of life, but expanding it. You don't have to spend a lot of money to eat well, look great, live in a nice house, and drive a decent car. If you are making an average income, all this can be done by learning how to spend money wisely.

For those of you who may be borrowing this book from a friend because you don't have the money to buy it, I understand how tough it can be at times. I hope that you, too, will be able to pick up some tips to make life a little better.

I don't talk a lot in this book about giving to God and to others, although it is a principle I believe in with all my heart. God somehow has a way of giving us back everything that we give to him when we contribute through our churches or give directly to his hurting, needy children.

With all my heart, I wish each of you a fun-filled, healthy, prosperous—although not necessarily wealthy—life.

1

MONEY: A TOOL FOR FAMILY FUN

Y ou'll never find any coins on the street here," Wendy said as we walked along the street in Waterloo, Belgium, a suburb of Brussels. "The Belgians pick them up."

About ten minutes later I reached down and picked up a Belgian fifty-franc piece, a coin worth about fifty cents. "What's this?" I asked her.

"I can't believe it. I've lived here six months, and I've never seen a coin on the street before."

The opposite is true here in the United States; almost every time I take a walk, I find a coin. I don't think most Americans would stop to pick up a penny, but we also don't pick up quarters, dimes, and nickels. And sometimes we lose paper money. In about a three-week span, I found a soggy five-dollar bill blown up against the trunk of a tree and, in the parking lot of a mall, three one-dollar bills folded together and threatening to blow away.

That's one way to find money for family fun, but it would take quite a long time to accumulate enough to buy a hamburger for each family member. No, when we're talking about finding money for family fun, we're talking about how to earn, budget, and save money. We're talking about how to get the maximum from every dollar, so there is some left for family fun.

I once heard a man say, "Don't always think in terms of satisfying your needs with money. There may be another way to meet them."

Over the years I've thought a lot about that statement. At the time I heard it, I was very poor. In time, I discovered that the man knew what he was talking about. I learned that fun can be free. I learned that if I helped my friend, she would help me, and both of us would have our needs met without spending money. I learned that because of our nation's affluent lifestyle, tons of possessions are given or thrown away every year—good things that could be recycled for my use.

I learned to accept with gratitude what people offered me for free. I learned that they gave it from hearts of love. They wanted me to have it, and if I accepted with a gracious "Thank you. I appreciate this," it was enough.

I learned never to look at an object with only its intended purpose in view. Often that item could be used in some other way to meet a need. A lace curtain not only looks beautiful at a window, it can also be used over a colored sheet as a very fancy tablecloth. Brightly colored golf tees can be glued together with wooden beads and other baubles to make colorful, inexpensive Christmas tree ornaments. Wheel rims from cars can be welded together to make stools and table bases for outdoor furniture.

It doesn't always take money or a lot of money to meet a need. I hope that by the time you finish reading this book, you will have a whole new way of looking at money, possessions, and your need of them.

A Money-Attitude Checkup

Someone once said, "We can never be too thin or too rich." And someone else, when asked how much money is enough, replied, "Just a little more than you have."

There is probably not a boy or girl, man or woman who does not know the truth of these two statements. When it comes to money, one does not meet too many satisfied people.

When a young couple is just starting out, they're glad to have only a few possessions, but very soon they want more possessions, then a bigger house and a better car, which means more income, which means the vicious cycle of demanding more and more money has begun.

A well-known national magazine recently told the story of two couples who began the cycle of need versus want. Everything went well for one couple until their first child arrived. Momma decided she didn't want to go back to work after the baby was born; she wanted to stay home and rear him. This is a very wise and good decision, but since the couple's life-style had been geared to two incomes, there was a time of radical adjustment. This couple is going to make it, since both are learning to cut back, do with less, wear it out, buy for less, use coupons, find it for free, and make vacations a time for visiting friends and grandparents, rather than taking expensive trips.

The second couple was also doing well, until the husband lost his job. They became credit-card junkies, pushing their credit limit to the hilt. They were in big trouble instantly. Of course, they had never thought of saving. They were young, healthy, had good jobs—no problem.

It took them some time to untangle their financial affairs, and to do it, they had to learn a new lifestyle of frugality, creativity, and carefulness. Oh, yes—the credit cards are gone. They retained one for emergencies, but that's all it's for—emergencies.

Everything in our national economy is geared to rampant consumerism. If it wasn't, the economy would probably collapse. Consumerism is what gives us all something to do, something to sell, somewhere to go to work.

Larry Burkett says, "The root problem of financial problems, with various alterations, is attitude. The attitude may be greed, covetousness, ignorance, indulgence, or impatience. Some people are ingenious enough to combine two or more of these attitudes, but the result is always the same: financial bondage."[1]

What we need to learn is balance with regard to money. We need to learn to be content with what we have and, at the same time, work to get better jobs and earn more pay. This is a difficult concept to adopt. The poverty-ridden certainly are not content with their financial status, and we can easily understand why. More difficult to understand is the lack of contentment found in the wealthy, whose consumption of tranquilizers, cars, houses, "things," tells us they are not satisfied, either. Everyone seems to be searching for more.

Don't misunderstand—money isn't bad. In fact, it's rather nice to have money. I learned when I was very poor that the longest time on record is the time between two paychecks. Trying to make a few dollars stretch until the next paycheck is hard work. Running completely out of money when there are little people in the house is scary business.

Money is good, and we need it. But we need to decide how much we actually need. We need to choose a life-style commensurate with our ability to earn money. Furthermore, we cannot love money and the things it can buy. In fact, we are warned in the Bible not to love money—not because money is bad, but because the *love of money* is an insatiable desire that can consume us and everything we value.

We need to view money as a tool—a tool for family fun. It takes money for a family to have fun. In some cases it only takes a little, and in other cases, quite a lot of money is required.

Start Simply

After I wrote my first book, *Raising Kids on Purpose for the Fun of It,*[2] someone asked me, "Gwen, how do you get teenagers to participate in family fun? Mine don't want to do anything with the rest of the family."

One way is to start with simple, inexpensive activities when the children are young and work your way up to more elaborate family adventures as they become older. The perfect vacation for a young child is sunshine, water, and you. A toddler doesn't understand Disneyland. In fact, some of the rides might terrify him. A young child doesn't need a lot to be happy, so don't give a lot. Don't desensitize a child with so much that when he or she is older, nothing makes an impression.

As the child grows older, up the ante. Offer more in terms of family fun. Miniature golf doesn't cost much. Simple amusement parks and zoos cost a little, but not a lot. There are hundreds of simple pleasures that are inexpensive. Watch your weekend newspapers, raid bookstore shelves for resource books, and talk to other parents to glean good ideas.

Then, when the child is in late childhood (preteen years), plan more elaborate family vacations. Now is a great time for a trip to Disneyland or Disney World. Now a trip to Sea World will mean more, because the child has learned about conservation and aquatic animals.

Save the truly big adventures for when your child becomes a teenager. Then is the time for a trip to Hawaii, a backpacking adventure in Canada, or parasailing in Mexico. If you've saved and haven't overspent on earlier family activities—if you've planned—you can probably pull off at least one great memory-making adventure for your kids.

I don't know too many teenagers, or even adult children, who will refuse an opportunity to go on a family vacation that has real appeal to them. But don't expect them to be excited about visiting great-aunt Millie for two weeks in July. They're not going to want to do it, and can you really blame them? Be truthful: How excited are you about that kind of vacation?

Balancing Spending and Saving

Some people like to save money. They prepare so well for a "rainy day" that there is never anything for a sunny today. While it is important to plan for the future, it is also important not to delay living in the present. It's difficult for most of us to achieve balance between spending and saving.

A friend of mine is married to a man who has had cancer in the past and therefore cannot get life insurance. They have taken care of the problem by faithfully setting aside a certain portion of their income and investing it. They never deviate from this path, for their future depends on it. But the portion they save still leaves them money for living now.

Long ago I read a most interesting book about a woman who had been very poor as a child. She married a rather wealthy man. When he died, she inherited his fortune and began to manage it. She became an astute businesswoman, but she refused to spend one cent of the principal or any of her investments. As time went on, she refused to spend money on anything but the bare necessities to keep body and soul together.

Eventually she died, alone, miserable, in an antiquated dress in a decaying old house. In the bank, she had an unbelievable fortune. *For what?* I asked myself. This was a story of greed, stinginess, and meanness. The woman lived for saving money, to the point of addiction. She drove away everyone who might have wanted some of her precious money, and she perished with no one to mourn her passing.

The point of the story is, *live now!* Plan for the future the best you can, but not to the extent that it robs you of the resources for providing quality family times now. At some point we have to trust God with the future, anyway. Why not start now?

Larry Burkett has written extensively on the subject of money and families. Without going into detail, he says God's plan for contentment is:

1. Establish a reasonable standard of living.
2. Establish a habit of giving.
3. Establish priorities.
4. Develop a thankful attitude.
5. Reject a fearful spirit.
6. Seek God's will for you.
7. Stand up to the fear (about money).
8. Trust God's promise.[3]

Budgets Are Back

Obviously, if we are going to control family saving and spending, we need a plan. That plan has a name that many of us hate—*budget.* In some families a budget becomes the ogre that destroys all fun, but it shouldn't. A budget is a plan for spending. It's a tool, not a slave master we serve. Budgets are there to serve us, to guide us, to help us have funds for family fun.

Perhaps family values are more apparent in a budget than anywhere else. Each family's goals and priorities are reflected here. One family will value sports events and equipment over every other kind of family activity. Another will spend heavily on books and compact discs. Yet another will live in a very simple house and spend their money on travel.

Every family's budget will be different; there is no right or wrong budget plan. What's right for your family is a plan that takes care of current needs and saves some for the future. We earn money so that we can spend it, and the decisions we make about how to spend it can and should provide for family security and family fun while our children are still living at home.

A budget can allow us to spend money without guilt. If we've budgeted to spend money on dinner out for the whole family, we can go and never wonder if we should be spending the money. Instead, we can kick back and really enjoy our dinner without guilt.

I'm not going to tell you how to make a budget. There are dozens of books and writers to help you do this. I have included some of these books in the bibliography at the end of this book. If you need advice on how to make a family budget, a visit to your local library should provide you with all the help you need.

Why Spend Money on Fun?

When you think back to your childhood, what stands out in your mind? Do you remember the color of the carpet in the living room? Was that carpet brand-new or threadbare? Did your family own the latest car? Do you remember the Easter outfit you wore when you were ten?

Perhaps you remember those things. I do, vaguely. But the important memories are of the fun times we had together as a family.

I remember when we would get together with my dad's brother and my mother's sister (who happened to be married to each other) and their children, my double cousins. We were four adults and eight children, bent on having a fun, crazy time together.

My aunt and uncle and my parents never had a lot of money available, but we always had fun when we were together. We often played crazy games—the adults playing right along with the children. How many clothespins could a person drop from four feet up into the neck of a milk bottle? We dressed up in costumes, using whatever was available in the closets, and put on plays for each other. We laughed and talked and giggled half the night. We didn't spend money; we just had fun and built a mountain of memories.

I remember another time when we spent just a little money for gas and the entrance fee to Yellowstone Park. We took two cars (absolutely essential with that crowd). My uncle's family set up a big tent, and our family slept in a homemade camper on the back of a pickup.

My grandmother accompanied us on that trip, and she slept in the tent. The first night, we sat around the campfire until we were too sleepy to keep our eyes open and then went to bed. Long after it should have been quiet, there was uproarious laughter coming from the tent. My mom, afraid she was missing out on all the fun, climbed out of the camper and padded over to the tent.

She had a little trouble finding the flap of the tent and was fumbling with it when she heard my grandmother scream. Mom didn't know about the conversation that had gone on inside the tent just moments before.

Yellowstone Park is noted for wildlife, and bears were a real campground nuisance. Someone had said to Grandma, "Grandma, we'll put you on the cot right in front of the door. Then if a bear comes, he'll get you first." My feisty, white-haired grandmother was laughing and striking back at the teasers when my mother began fumbling with the tent flap. Grandmother thought a bear was trying to get into the tent, and her scream just about frightened my mother to death.

18

On that same trip my uncle's car would heat lock every time it stopped. It also had a driver's-side window that couldn't be rolled up. Everyone stopped to feed the bears back then, and every time they did, the car would heat lock. I was in the backseat when a big black bear stuck its head in the window to see if we had food. The whole window opening was full of bear head, and my crazy uncle backed across the seat, practically into my aunt's lap, to take a picture of the bear—close up!

All of this to illustrate that children won't remember or care if their home has the latest of everything. They will remember the happy fun—even the crazy times—they had with you, their parents. That's why we spend money on family fun. Spending money to buy family memories is one of the best investments you can make.

Family Adventures for Little or No Money

🐾 Give each child a limited amount of money and take him to a swap meet, thrift store, or garage sale. Challenge him to see how many treasures he can get for his money.

🐾 Take a hike and see what nature will provide for craft projects. Look for interesting branches, mosses, leaves, flowers, stones, pods, and so forth. When you get home, help the children arrange their treasures.

🐾 Visit a beach or stream bank. Take along a shovel, empty soup cans, a funnel, and empty milk cartons. Use these to build a fine sand castle, then pretend you are the ladies, knights, kings, and queens who live in the castle. Make up your own story, or bring along a book.

🐾 Make sock puppets by putting a rubber band around the toe of a sock, then turning it so the rubber band is on the inside. Decorate the sock with eyes, glasses,

---

19

teeth, lips, and so forth. Peel-off labeling material is excellent for making the puppet's features. Show your children how to put their hand inside and make the puppet talk. Have a puppet show, using one of their favorite stories and their homemade puppets.

🐦 Take a walk through a garden or an area where flowers are grown for seeds or bulbs. Perhaps you'll see, as we once did, a whole hillside covered with iris, or miles and miles of tulips forming a huge patchwork, or a garden where exotic and wonderful roses abound. Have the children vote on the most beautiful flower they see.

🐦 Attend ethnic food-tasting events. In our area, communities frequently have food fairs where all kinds of wonderful treats are available. The cost is minimal.

🐦 Plant a vegetable garden together. Seeds are inexpensive, but the experience of learning to grow plants is invaluable. Best of all, the time the child spends with you is priceless. If the child is small, invest in some child-size tools, so he or she is not stymied by adult-size implements.

🐦 Rent a rowboat or a paddleboat for an hour. Teach your children to row. Rent or borrow a canoe and learn about canoe safety. Take a ferryboat ride. Have a meal aboard the ferry; watch for aquatic life; look at the city's skyline from this very different viewpoint.

🐦 Go to the top of a tall building that has an observation deck. Help the children identify familiar landmarks from this height. Give a prize to the one who gets the most right.

🐦 Hang a sheet across a doorway and have a shadow play. Put a light on the actors' side to project their shadows onto the sheet. A fun thing to do is pretend to perform surgery, removing various items from "the patient"—the more absurd the item, the funnier.

❧ Go on a family bike ride. If you don't have bikes for everyone, you can rent them. Many families invest in bikes, because bike riding is such an excellent family activity. More and more safe bike trails are being developed each year.

❧ Tour a factory. If the factory will not give a tour for a small group, join together with other neighborhood families. We've toured cheese factories, candy factories, cereal factories, meat-packing plants, aircraft manufacturers, pulp paper mills, and newspaper printing plants. There are probably a number of interesting factories in your area.

❧ National historic monuments and parks are inexpensive and provide abundant learning opportunities for families. When my brothers and I were in high school, they worked on a turn-of-the-century ranch that is now a national historic monument—the Grant Kohrs Ranch in Deer Lodge, Montana. This is only one of hundreds of such places set aside to preserve our national history.

❧ House tours are fun for older children. The houses of famous and not-so-famous Americans are scattered about the country. Thomas Jefferson's and John Adams' houses are in Virginia, Molly Brown's house is in Denver. Visit Vizcaya in Miami, the William Randolph Hurst house in San Simeon, California, the Vanderbilt mansions (one in Hyde Park, New York, and another in Asheville, North Carolina). There are hundreds of once-private homes now open to the public. Entrance fees are minimal, and the history learned through a visit is amazing.

2

HOW DO WE GET THE MONEY WE NEED?

I loved the television commercial that said, "We get money the old-fashioned way. We earn it." Contrary to the thinking of some people today, who try lotteries, sweepstakes, and many other high-risk, low-pay activities, the best way to get money is to earn it.

Not long ago I was in a shopping mall near a major university. A young panhandler asked me for money. I looked at him and saw that he was able-bodied and seemingly of reasonable intelligence. I couldn't resist asking him why he wanted the money. "To buy an ice-cream cone," he said. That was more than I could let go by, and so I told him, "You'll have to get money the way I did—by working for it." Needless to say, that was the end of our conversation.

You cannot get something for nothing. As authors Ron and Judy Blue tell us, "Even in the simplest economic system, one thing of value is traded for something else of equal value. Value is in the mind of the beholder, and the price merely reflects the value. For example, one person may trade a day's labor for one hundred dollars, and another person may trade a day's labor for something more or less. One person may trade many days of labor for an automobile, and others may trade those same days of labor for a vacation. The 'value' of that trade-off is in the eye of the beholder."[1]

Money is the tangible thing we get from the hours we spend employed, and for most of us, work consumes a good portion of our waking hours. If this is true, it's important that we work at jobs that bring us adequate monetary rewards. This may be easier said than done. If we are not making enough money at the job we now have, we need to take some action: Find a new job, retrain for a better job, relocate to a part of the country where the pay is better.

Most of us don't have to be employed very long before we discover it's easier to work at a job if it brings us a sense of satisfaction, of personal value, as well as adequate compensation. A job can give us a sense of status, of respect, of purpose, and a way to make a meaningful contribution to society.

A Quick History of Work

During a recent visit to the newly restored Ellis Island, I was fascinated by the history of work in America depicted through photographic displays. Because many Europeans were near starvation in their homelands as a result of unemployment, epidemics, and an economic downturn in Europe, they fled to the new country of the United States in hope of finding better jobs. Stories of economic prosperity were sent back to the Old World, with the result that some people believed the streets of America were lined with gold.

The earliest immigrants, however, did not find golden streets. Their first introduction to the New World was often roughness, cursing, intimidation, and blackmail that began the moment they landed. The restaurant on Ellis Island was called a den of thieves because of the underhanded activities going on there. Even there on the island, some who changed European currency into American dollars extracted up to 75 percent of the value of an immigrant's money.

For employment, what most of the immigrants found were low-paying jobs with interminable hours. Women and children worked like slaves in factories and cottage industries. Children were often put in the most dangerous places in the factories, since they were considered dispensable.

An Ellis Island picture caption about working women says:

> Many immigrant women had to earn money to help support their families. The vast majority stayed at home, but to make ends meet they often took in laundry, sewing, or boarders, or helped run a family business. Women who worked outside the home usually entered domestic services, but some also worked as farm laborers, factory hands, or mill workers. Employers often hired women because they cost less than male workers.
>
> In the late 1800s and early 1900s, social reformers pressed for laws protecting women from exploitation. By 1912, thirty-nine states had enacted legislation limiting the number of hours women could work in a day. Though a step in the right direction, the shorter day meant a significant wage cut for many immigrant women, who had worked the extra hours to provide their households with necessities.

Men did not have an easy time of it, either. They worked at hard labor for minimum wages. Life was very difficult for these European immigrants. In some ways it seemed unfair that they came to escape poverty and hardship and immediately found more of the same.

Many of us (approximately 40 percent of our ancestors entered the country through Ellis Island) can trace our ancestry through Ellis Island and other "portals of opportunity." Our forebears came here to work, and work they did. America was the land of opportunity. Most immigrants found work in the New World. Even though the pay was meager and the labor arduous, they did have a chance at a new life. Most of them survived the hardships and became part of the economic bedrock of this nation; some even went on to become very successful.

The United States is still a land of great opportunity, and although some may dispute that the great opportunities of the past still exist, we have as much or more than any country on earth to offer those who are willing and able to work.

One Income versus Two

Many families today feel they can't make it financially with only one income. It is true that the exorbitant cost of real estate makes it difficult, if not impossible, for a family with one income to purchase a house. Furthermore, if you want to give your children the advantage of a college education, it's almost imperative that two parents and the child work to make it happen.

Over the last few years, women have entered the work force in record numbers. A *Time* magazine cover story on working women said, "In 1960 . . . 34.8% of women were in the work force, in contrast to 57.8% today. The number of female lawyers and judges has climbed from 7,500 to 180,000 today, female doctors from 15,672 to 108,200 and female engineers from 7,404 to 174,000. The number of women elected to office has more than tripled since 1975 at the local level, though their presence has barely changed in the U.S. Congress."[2]

The article gave an interesting perspective on the history of working women: "Not all the changes were the result of feminist ideology. Female employment in the U.S. has been rising since the 1890s. . . . The sole exceptions to these trends occurred in the 1950s, when, in the prosperous aftermath of World War II, motherhood and babymaking became a kind of national cult: there was a return to earlier marriage, families were bigger and divorce rates stabilized. Though women continued to pour into the workplace during the '50s, this fact was blotted out by the decade's infatuation with blissful domesticity."[3]

What Does It Cost for a Mother to Work?

No one will dispute that women are employed outside their homes in record numbers. Added income is in some cases a necessity, and in others a pleasant option. But the costs of a mother of young and school-age children working need to be weighed against the actual monetary gains. As in everything else in life, full-time employment outside the home for a working mother has its pros and cons, its pluses and minuses. Every economist cautions that working mothers will not be making as much as they had expected, when they take into consideration the cost of clothing, lunches, transportation, child care, and increased income taxes.

Working mothers must analyze their goals. They must weigh the value of the extras their income can provide against the price their children will pay for not having them there when they need them, plus the price of exhaustion at the end of a day that often leaves little strength to attend to family needs.

It would be best, if at all possible, to find another way to meet your family's needs instead of returning to work when your children are still young. For some, this is impossible, and no blame or guilt need be accepted by a woman who must work to support her family.

When my children were small, I had to decide whether to find a job or to stay home and make the best of it financially. This was during a time when we were very poor. I decided to try and get by without working for as long as I could, so that I could be with my young children. I wanted to be there when my baby took his first step. I wanted to hear his first words. I wanted to help my little girl learn to ride a bike and sew her first project. What mother doesn't?

It was tough. Life would have been much easier, from a monetary standpoint, if I had taken a job. But we made it through that time, and now, looking back, I'm glad I didn't go to work then. I'm glad I was there for them, and I am thankful that we were able to work it out. Not everyone can.

Becoming a two-income family should be a family decision, because, done properly, it will involve every member of the family helping with housework, school conferences, transportation, and a multitude of other activities. When your family makes the decision that Mom should go to work, that decision can either bring the family closer as it works together for common goals, or split it apart.

If you've thought through what it will mean for your family to be a two-income family, if you've planned how the money earned will be dispersed, if you've talked through the implications in terms of who is going to do the housework, and have decided it's right for you to go to work, then do it.

For me, going back to work when my children were older not only provided necessary funds for family goals, but also gave me an outlet for my creative energies. I had the total support of my family. Although the children were old enough to fend for themselves, I kept a careful eye on our son Mark's whereabouts and activities. It was Mark I was most concerned about (he was in junior high), and he cast the deciding vote when he said, "Mom, it's what you always wanted to do. Go for it."

I have to be honest and say that I didn't allocate household chores the way I should have, and the result was exhaustion and near-total burnout. From my own experience, I would caution you to give this matter serious consideration. No woman on earth can carry two full-time jobs for very long without something giving way—her attitude, her health, or her sanity.

Kids Can Work, Too

I remember when Mark took his first job as a busboy in a local Mexican restaurant. He cleaned tables, served coffee, and swept the floor. He had to wear a white shirt, black slacks and shoes, and a green apron. His clothes reeked of Mexican food by the end of the day, and the tomato stains were nearly impossible to get out of his clothing.

In this particular restaurant, waiters shared their tips with the busboys. When one prospered, they all did. And although the wages weren't great, there were some Saturdays when Mark brought home $75 in tips for the day.

But perhaps more important was the fact that Mark felt good about himself. Although he truly was not suited for restaurant work, still he had a job and he was doing it well. He also was able to buy his own clothing and pay for his own entertainment.

Most important of all, he was gaining a valuable commodity—work experience. His next job was as a teller in a bank. He's worked there for five years and is now a bookkeeper and is considering a position where he will be trained in investments.

It's important that teens contribute to the financial needs of the family. Whereas once young people's wages were, of necessity, turned over to the family, in our modern life, teens' work will largely benefit them. Those early youthful immigrant workers probably did not pocket their earnings, but rather handed them over to their parents to help make ends meet.

Working can serve another purpose besides making money. As teens experience a variety of jobs, they have the opportunity to find out what they truly enjoy doing. Part-time jobs can be one way for a child to find direction for the future.

There is an interesting book titled *Summer Jobs: Finding Them, Getting Them, Enjoying Them.*[4] This is a handbook of ideas and how-to tips for high school and college students. In the book the author, Sandra Schocket, lists agencies, opportunities, specific fields, and resources for alternative job options.

As I thumbed through the resources, a couple of listings caught my eye: "Strategies for Getting an Overseas Job" and "Work Your Way Around the World." Doesn't that sound like fun? Wouldn't we all like to be that young and free again?

A word of caution probably is needed here. Some teens cannot handle both school and a job. Priorities must enter into the picture. Which is more important—the teen's education or making money? In most cases, schoolwork probably needs to be a priority.

In a recent discussion with a friend who is a college professor, I heard her complain about the apathetic attitude of the students. "The students are different than they used to be. They are less motivated to study—less goal oriented—less ambitious. Of course," she added, "many of them work twenty-five to thirty hours a week just to stay in school. They are too tired to study when the time comes." There's something radically wrong with this picture. Why send a child to college only to have him be too tired to study because he is working too much?

If a job is interfering with a teen's ability to handle the rest of his life, perhaps a formal job should be deferred until school is finished. He can still take casual work such as baby-sitting, yard cleanup, or car washing—jobs that allow him to say no when his studies demand his time and attention. He can cer-

29

tainly help out at home and smooth the path for others in the family who are working.

If such is the case, the nonworking teen needs to feel that his contribution is important. It is! He needs to feel good about himself. He's not dumb or stupid because he cannot handle everything at once. If he can't handle it all, he's still all right. Perhaps he should be encouraged to make full use of his summers and other vacation times for employment, so work and school are not in competition for his time. It's a matter of priorities, and there is no better time than the teen years to learn how to choose among the multitude of opportunities available to each of us.

Is Part-time Work Best?

This is a question that's being asked by both women and men. A *USA Today* article tells about Mats Brenner, a mathematician from Bloomington, Minnesota, who's decided part-time work is best for his family. Mats works for Honeywell just four days a week. The rest of the week he plays with his kids. Mary, his wife, also works four days a week at Honeywell as a scientist.

"I view it [part-time work] as a viable way to work and advance, while still finding time for other pursuits, most recently, caring for my children," says Charlene Canape, wife, mother of two children, writer, and former editor of *Business Week,* in her book *The Part-time Solution.*[5]

In 1986, *Working Woman* magazine found that part-time working mothers were more content with their lives than all other working women. Although it is possible to work full-time at a career and manage to keep up with everything else, one needs to ask the questions, "Is it worth the struggle? Could there be another way?" Part-time work for one or both parents can be a solution with happy results. There are advantages and disadvantages to part-time work, and both men and women need to look at them.

Advantages

Part-time work gives you more hours at home, since part-time can mean anything from ten to thirty-nine hours a week. Most part-time jobs are twenty to thirty hours a week. There are all kinds of ways to put these hours together. A great advantage can be gained if the hours can be bunched together on set days, rather than spreading a few hours a day throughout a work week. Three eight-hour days will probably give you more time at home than five four-and-one-half-hour days, simply because you have to get ready and commute to work only three times, rather than five.

However you put it together, twenty-four hours of employment rather than forty is going to give you more time at home.

Part-time work gives you more energy to work at home. Less commuting and less stress are bound to give you more energy. Often the kind of work done at home is different from your employment, and the change can be energizing.

Part-time work gives independence. While their children are young, many women do not want to return to full-time jobs. At the same time, they may have become used to having their own money and making decisions about how to spend that money. They enjoy working, but they also want to be there to meet their children's needs. For many, this dilemma can be solved by working part-time.

Child-care arrangements may be easier for part-time workers. In some part-time situations, parents may be able to arrange their schedules in such a way that child care is covered by the flexibility of both parents' schedules. If it is not, it may be easier to find someone to care for the child a few days a week or a few hours a day than it is to find a caretaker for a full work week.

Part-time provides a way to experiment with occupations. Part-time work provides both teenagers and parents with an opportunity to see what kinds of jobs are available and how they might fit into those jobs. Part-time work can give you the opportunity to look for a different or more rewarding type of work.

It used to be that people trained for a job and stayed in it for the rest of their lives, but that is not the case today. Now people may retrain four or five times and start new careers at any time in their lives. It's part of what makes being alive today so great! If you hate your job, do something else. Retrain! Rethink your whole approach to work! Start your own business!

31

Part-time work is a way to maintain Social Security and other benefits. Many women who don't want to work full-time work part-time just to maintain their Social Security or benefits from the company where they have been previously employed.

Part-time work can provide an escape from routine housework. A part-time job can get you out of the house for a few hours a week and thereby break the monotony. The only problem is that many part-time jobs are also monotonous. Take a good look before you leap.

Disadvantages

There are also some disadvantages to be weighed in all of this. Part-time jobs don't pay much, unless your line of work is highly skilled and there is great demand for it. It is wise, as in all jobs, to weigh what you will get in income against what it will cost you to work—clothes, child care, transportation, social obligations, and so forth.

Part-time employment is on the rise, and one of the reasons is that if employees work under a certain number of hours, employers don't have to pay benefits. With the high cost of benefits, many employers are hiring multiple part-timers and still getting their work done. If benefits are important to you, this is something to consider. Ask these questions about benefits:

1. What about vacation? Will I be paid for it?
2. Which holidays will I be paid for?
3. Do I build up sick leave?
4. When raises and promotions come, will I be considered in the same way full-time employees are?
5. Will it bother me that I start a project and because I am part-time someone else will finish it?
6. What will the attitude of my co-workers and boss be? Will they feel that I am not part of the organization because I am not on the full-time staff?

In addition to considering these questions, you need to know that your own attitude can work against you. An attitude that says, "I'm only a part-timer, so therefore I should be able to do my housework and yardwork without any help," opens the possibility of your coming under enough stress to sink the ship. If you work part-time, you are still a working person, with all the stresses accompanying that role.

You do need help. You need help at least from your family. You may need help from a nanny, a housekeeper, or a gardener. You may also need a break from your children, the same way your full-time working sisters and brothers do. It is possible, if you cultivate an attitude in which you fail to take care of yourself, to end up more worn-out than a full-time worker.

If you decide that part-time work is the way for you and your family to go, here are some more points to consider:

1. Decide which hours of the week would be best for you to work. As long as you'll be working part-time, you might as well try to find a job that best fits into your schedule.

2. When deciding hours, think about child-care factors. Is there a way to juggle child care so that you can hang on to some of the money you make and don't have to pay it all to a day-care center?

3. Are you a morning or an evening person? Could you find a job that fits in with your makeup? Do you want to give your best hours to your job or to your family? When you've answered these questions, start looking for a job you can do during your prime time—the time when you are most awake, most productive, most efficient. Or save the prime time for your family and find a job that doesn't take the best of you, leaving you with little to give your family.

4. Do you want to work a little every day or a couple of full days? Do you want to get ready to go to work and commute in traffic every day, or could you go to work two or three days a week and be just as happy?

33

Is Working at Home the Answer?

There is a strong trend today to work at home. The trend has, in part, been created by electronic technology. When an employee plugs a modem into a computer and a phone line, the ability to communicate with others online is the same as if he were in the company's building. A facsimile (FAX) machine makes it possible to see a document almost as quickly as if you walked down the hall to a colleague's office. With advanced telephone communication systems, the person you want to talk with is only a few dialed digits away. I don't know about your office, but in the ones where I have worked, employees call each other even if they are only twenty feet away, so it makes little difference if the calling employee is twenty or more miles away.

Large corporations realize their employees produce more work of better quality when they are not distracted by conversation, ringing telephones, drop-of-the-hat meetings, coffee breaks, and so forth. They also know that their employees are going to produce better work if they don't have to spend hours on the freeway or in a train, commuting to and from work. Thus the trend to at-home work stations.

That's one way of working at home, but there are others. Many small businesses are begun in homes to keep overhead costs down. Do not get the mistaken idea that these are part-time jobs. They can be all-consuming in terms of time and energy. Getting a small business launched is probably one of the most taxing ventures anyone can set out to do. You don't establish a home-based business to make big money, either. In the beginning there is little money. In fact, often the owner of the business may be fortunate to get any salary at all. Cash flow is a problem that often continues to haunt small businesses for many years.

However, if a home-based business is to succeed, it will have to become profitable sooner or later, and sooner is much better than later.

Some types of home-based businesses are word processing, insurance claim work, editing, writing, child care, home beauty shops, mail-order work, consulting, and photography. There are books in your local library that will give you lots of ideas for home-based businesses.

There are important points to consider before starting a home-based business. Find a place to work that can be dedicated strictly to that function. You need a place to spread out your projects and not have to pick them up at the end of every day. It would be great if that room had a door with a lock.

Avoid distractions. It's easy to be distracted by housework and projects around the house. "Well, I'll just stick a load of clothes in the washer. It will only take another minute or so to load the dishwasher." Before you know it, your time is all eaten away.

Prepare for isolation. Recently I talked with a writer friend who had gone home several years ago to free-lance. "How's it going?" I asked.

"Oh, Gwen, I just couldn't stand the isolation any longer. I've gone back to work in an editorial office."

I understood, for I had just gone through the longest, darkest winter of my life, one in which the isolation nearly incapacitated me. I learned that working out of your home may be all right for some people to do occasionally. For other people, it may even be all right to do every day. But I needed people.

Decide how many hours a week you can work. Can you put in a full work week from your home? Will you be able to discipline yourself to stay at it that many hours a day?

Count the costs of setting up. Equipment is expensive. Just what will you need, and how much will it cost?

How much can you afford to lose? What if it doesn't work out and you lose money on your home-based business? What happens if you become ill? Can you survive until you are strong enough to work again?

Check out insurance needs. Can you get insurance that is adequate to your needs if you are self-employed? What will it cost you?

Think about who's going to take care of the business side of your business. Who's going to fill out the legal and tax forms? Do you need an accountant? a lawyer? You probably need both.

What do you need in salary? If you are free-lancing for a company other than your own, you probably won't be paid a salary, but will be paid either by the project or on an hourly basis. Will that work for you? If you are paid by the project, do you need to set it up so that part of your earnings come in at the beginning, part in the middle, and part at the end of the project?

Pay attention, and don't be misled. Last, and very important, be wary of scams. There are all kinds of people promising all kinds of things for home-based businesses. Usually they want you to buy some kind of kit or make some kind of investment (often sizable) to start your business. *Be careful!*

There are all kinds of ways to get the money we need. No one way is right or wrong. You, and only you, can decide what is best for your family. It's an exciting time in history, because there are so many work opportunities. There is also an attitude that says it's all right to experiment and look around at different employment options, both when you are just entering the work force and later, when you may have become established in a profession.

Work is the best way to get the money we need, and since we have to work, it's best that we give serious consideration to our training, attitude, work style, and place of employment.

Marsha Sinetar, who writes on the subject of work, says:

> There are hundreds of thousands of people who have overcome both internal and external obstacles to become successful doing work they love. If people can cultivate self-respect and inner security and develop a commitment to their own talents, they can earn as much money as they need, or want. This is true success.
>
> The task is easier than people imagine. All it takes is everything they have to give: all their talent, energy, focus, commitment and all their love. The rewards are worth it and are evident the minute one consciously chooses on behalf of his or her own values, inclinations and vision.[6]

The secret to earning money for your family by doing work that is enjoyable and meaningful is in making choices about what kind of work is best for you and your family, in taking risks to do that work, and in going on with life, no matter what the outcome of those actions. So choose! Risk! Get on with life, today!

Family Adventures for Little or No Money

🐦 Arrange a tour of a printing plant and see the high-speed equipment in action.

🐦 Visit a shop or factory where candy is made. The children will love the samples.

🐦 Visit a TV or radio studio that offers tours or seats for a show's taping.

🐦 Check your local library for story times, or start one in your own neighborhood.

🐦 Go to a fish hatchery to see fingerlings or migrating fish.

🐦 Take turns planning and cooking meals. The cook gets to make anything he or she wants for dinner, the family eats it without complaint (this may take some supervision!).

🐦 Set goals for family cleanup chores. Who can clean his or her room the fastest? How long did it take to clean up after dinner last night? Can we better that time today?

3

TEACH YOUR CHILDREN ABOUT MONEY

If you're a parent, put this resolution on your . . . list: I will raise financially responsible kids," says Mary Rowland in an article syndicated by the *New York Times*.[1]

That's a great goal, but how do we go about attaining it?

"Children need real-world experience, not just explanation, on which to base their understanding," suggests Sylvia C. Chard, co-author of *Engaging Children's Minds: The Project Approach*.[2]

The best way to teach your children your values with regard to money (and everything else) is to be with them, talk to them, give them real-world experience in handling money.

Talk about Money

In many families, money is a taboo subject. For some reason, parents don't want their children to know how much they make or how they spend their money. Perhaps they are afraid their children will pass on the information to the neighbors or others. Some think children can't handle the information, especially if the family is struggling financially. So many children grow up financially illiterate.

Mary Rowland says, "If you expect your children to be able to function as adults, they must know how to earn, spend, save, borrow and invest. The sooner you start teaching, the better."[3]

About a year ago, a couple in Kirkland, Washington, launched a system to help parents teach their children about handling money. The system is called "BanKit," and its symbol is a pig— Hamilton Hawg ("a real cool critter"). Hamilton's picture is on the very attractive box cover, and it is he who gives the kids instructions about banking and money management in a child's manual. Hamilton explains all about banks, checks, deposit slips, the check register, and other banking functions. He tells the children, "Managing money is like playing a video game, to be a winner it takes practice and a good strategy. . . . In developing your Super Strategy we will look at both earning and spending." He calls the two parts of his Super Strategy *Power Earning* and *Power Spending*.

Even though it had just been released, the kit won the coveted Parent's Choice Award for 1990 and the acclaim of the organization's president, Diana Huss Green. Parent's Choice reviews children's media—books, videos, movies, audio recordings, toys, music computer programs, and so forth.

BanKit is a teaching device to be used by both parents and children. It shows that managing your money can be fun. Using make-believe paperwork and designating the parent as the banker, BanKit shows children how to deposit and withdraw money, balance checkbooks, record transactions, and make decisions about spending and saving.

With the system, it is possible to give a child an allowance without money ever changing hands. The child merely issues a deposit slip to the parent for the agreed amount of the allowance. The transaction is recorded by the banker parent. It is easy to see how never having the money in hand in the first place might be a deterrent to spending it all the first day.

I asked one of the creators what she felt were the major advantages to the family that uses BanKit. She said:

1. It teaches the child responsibility for money management.
2. It raises the child's self-esteem because he can handle his own money.
3. It helps him make decisions about spending and saving.
4. It takes the burden off the parent.

When a child asks the parent, "Can I have it?" the answer is, "Do you have enough money?" It's as simple as that. The child learns that none of us can have everything we want. He also learns that if he wants something badly enough, he will have to work and save for it.

With 52,000 kits sold in a little more than a year, somebody thinks the Schweikerts' idea of teaching children to manage money is right on track. (The kit costs $29.95 and is available from BanKit, KidCorp Inc., P.O. Box 3268, Kirkland, WA 98083-3268.)

Teach Your Children about Budgets

Sylvia Porter, in one of her last books written before her death, said, "Budgets are back in style." They are now more important than ever, because of the rising cost of everything. When costs rise and income does not, there needs to be a plan for spending and saving money.

She has these suggestions about children and budgeting:

1. Begin giving your child an allowance just as soon as he or she understands the use of money for getting the things he or she wants.
2. Have an understanding about what the allowance is to cover. At first it may relate only to such things as toys and special treats, but adjustments should be made from time to time in the size of the allowance, and hence in its use. Many teenage boys and girls can handle allowances that cover their clothing. By the time they are mature, they will have had some experience in looking ahead and saving for special things.

3. In addition to having a clear understanding with your child on just what an allowance is or is not supposed to cover, renegotiate the contract at least once a year, to take new obligations into account.

4. Make your child's allowance a fair share in terms of your family's consumption in general.

5. Take into account what your child's friends and school-mates have. The allowance certainly should not be so much lower that the child feels constantly deprived, but it also should not be greatly in excess of what others get.

6. As your child gets older, give him a voice in deciding what his allowance should be. Let him share in a family round table on the spending plan. He will thus gain a greater appreciation of fair sharing.

7. Give your child full responsibility for spending his allowance, although your advice may be required for some things and should be available at all times. If he makes mistakes, he should take responsibility for them and put up with the results. In unusual situations you might help him out with an advance from the next week's allowance.

8. While your child is learning to plan ahead, give him the allowance to only cover short periods. Perhaps give first enough for the day, then for the week, and only later for somewhat longer periods. Very early in their lives, your children should learn where the family's money comes from and the effort that goes into earning it. A child's spending should, therefore, be made in part dependent on his own efforts. Children often can be taught the sim-ple lessons of earning and spending by being paid extra for special household tasks. But do not carry this too far. Your child may acquire the habit of putting all helpful-ness on a "pay me" basis. Pay only for exceptional, not routine, household chores. Do not confuse this sort of payment with the allowance.

9. Teenagers are notorious nonsavers. They tend to spend income as fast as possible and often on apparently friv-

olous things. But at the same time they are deeply attracted by such big-ticket items as motorcycles, autos, and stereos. Once a teenager sets an expensive item as a goal, the message usually seeps through that the purchase requires saving over a long period. Encourage your youngster to keep a savings goal within reasonable limits and not to make it a prolonged drudgery. Encourage your youngster also to learn how to manage a checking or savings account.

Porter quotes some guidelines developed by Household Finance Corporation on what children in various age brackets might be expected to buy and pay for out of their allowances:

Under 6: candy, gum, ice cream, small toys, gifts for others, books, playthings, paints, crayons, blocks, and dolls

Ages 6–9: movies, amusements, toys, books, magazines, hobbies, club dues, special savings for sports equipment, carfare and lunches at activities, school expenses, gifts for birthdays and holidays, and contributions

Ages 9–12: fees for skating rinks, pools, etc., club dues, hobby materials, sports equipment and repairs, games and special events, carfare and lunches at school, gifts for birthdays and holidays, contributions, trips, school supplies, clothing, and upkeep

Ages 12–18: the above, plus money for dates, grooming, cosmetics, jewelry, clothing, school activities, savings for special purposes such as travel and a future education.[4]

There are a lot of varied opinions about children and allowances. Some say that tying money to chores teaches children manipulation: "I'll only help if I'm paid." Those who feel this way say it is better to give them the money with no strings attached, as a means of teaching them money management. In that case, the allowance should never be taken away as punishment and it should never be withheld because some chore was not accomplished. Others feel there is no free ride (allowance) and children should work for money.

If you advocate an allowance, give children the rules before you give them the money. Tell them how you expect them to use the money. Sit down with them as soon as they are old enough to read and help them figure out their own rudimentary budget.

Know before you start that they will overspend, make unwise purchases, and fail, *but* sometimes they will succeed far beyond your expectations. Different children handle money differently. You may very well have one spender and one saver in your family. It sometimes becomes the parents' responsibility to protect the saver, since spenders have a way of going to the savers for money. If such is the case, you may well end up bailing out the spender, or you will have some interfamily loaning going on, which usually doesn't work too well.

Teach Your Child about the Family Budget

It is important to let a child see how the family's money is earned and spent. If possible, let him go to work with Mom or Dad once in a while. Let him see that it takes a lot of hours of work to get the money the family spends. Let him take part in deciding how the family's money will be spent.

It is impossible to achieve any control over a family's spending if goals are not clear. Most family's goals will be closely tied to money. Money will be spent first on those things the family values most. For some families, recreation will be a high priority. For others, the house they live in or the car they drive is very important. Some make education the top priority for the family. No one can tell your family what its goals should be and how you should spend your money. These are highly individualized decisions. The concern here is that enough time and thought be put into the decision-making process.

Larry Burkett, in a book called *The Complete Financial Guide for Young Couples,* advises parents to consider three fundamental principles that are applicable to everyone, parents *and* children.

44

First, teach your children that God owns everything by allowing them to see this principle in your lives. Be willing to put aside your own indulgences to meet needs in other people's lives. Begin to pray about the material needs you have, and let God provide them without borrowing, so your children can see that God is real.

Second, exercise self-discipline. There's no way that parents can establish financial discipline in their children if they themselves are undisciplined. In a practical way, this may be as simple as sharing your budget with your children to show them how you save to buy clothes, repair your car, and take vacations. Too often our children are led to believe that money really does grow on trees and all we have to do is pick some off when we need it. To allow your children to live this fantasy is to invite disaster when they're adults.

Parents need to practice moderation, regardless of their ability to generate income. God's instructions require that we exercise discipline in everything we do. It's easy to rationalize indulgence and lavishness under the "live like the King's kid" philosophy. If you believe that, look at the examples in God's Word. First, observe the King and see if he ever lived lavishly. Second, look at the men that Christ poured his life into and see if they did. And third, look at the apostle Paul's example. You don't have to live in poverty to serve Christ, but self-discipline and moderation are the rules.

Third, Burkett suggests you teach your children that everybody needs to live on a budget. It doesn't matter whether you make $8,000 a year or $800,000 a year; you need a budget.[5]

He suggests a four-part budget plan for children: 10 percent for giving, 40 percent for spending, 25 percent for long-term spending, 25 percent for surplus (a standby reserve fund).

Burkett feels most children should have some jobs around the house for which they are paid. They should also have some nonpaying jobs that they do because they are part of the family. He offers some ideas for paying children ages one to ten:

1. Pay them only for the jobs completed.
2. Pay them only for quality work.

3. Pay fairly and in line with your budget.

4. Use charts to help motivate young children do their work.

5. Teach them to share, using principles from God's Word.

6. Teach them to save.

For children ages eleven and above, Burkett feels earnings should be related to performance. He feels there has to be a strict performance code for teenagers' work. He says the teen years are the best time to learn timeliness, dependability, attitude, and honor.

When teens exhibit extra effort or do a superior job, then their work should receive an extra reward. They then come to understand the "better-work, better-pay" principle.

By this time in their life, teens should be operating from a budget. Like it or not, there is not an unlimited supply of funds to meet their needs and wants. They must learn to control spending, to save for the future, to give to others, and to have some money on hand for unexpected expenses.[6]

Teach Them to Give to God

God set up a principle of giving and receiving that works. Children need to learn how to give to God at a very early stage of life. They need to learn to give for the sheer joy of giving, not because they expect something in return.

The best way to teach your children to have a generous spirit of giving, whether to the Lord or to others, is to set an example. They need to see you preparing your offering and placing it in the collection basket. They need you to share from God's Word on the principles of giving. They need to hear you tell personal stories of God's faithfulness to your family.

There is a principle in Scripture of giving 10 percent of our earnings to God. Parents may force their children to give this amount from their earnings or allowance, but it is probably unwise to do so. Children can be encouraged to give, and they should be instructed about the principle of tithing.

Ten percent is the minimum. Giving begins to get exciting when we give sacrificially. God is not in the habit of failing those who cast themselves upon him and trust in his goodness.

Teach Them to Give to Others

It is important to teach our children to give to others. This can begin very early, when we allow little ones to give gifts to others. Some of their gifts may be rather simple, and they may be given to you. Every child picks a bouquet of dandelions and brings them to a parent. As parents, we need to accept gifts from our children just as they are offered, with love, gratitude, and attention.

As a means of teaching about giving and sharing, some families donate money to support a disadvantaged child from a foreign country. Glen and Dorothy thought supporting a child through a reputable organization was a good way to teach their three daughters about giving to others. For a number of years they sent money for the upkeep of "their child." In return they received notes and pictures.

The oldest of the three girls, Sherrill, spent a year in Finland as an exchange student. There she saw that although Finland has a high standard of living, people don't have all the things we consider necessary for our way of life: cars, electric dryers, dishwashers, and so forth. She began to realize that if Finnish people did not have all these items, people in third world countries had even less.

During her first year in college, Sherrill adopted, via an agency, an African boy. She began sending fifteen dollars a month for his upkeep. Fifteen dollars a month isn't a huge sum of money, unless you are a struggling college student. She managed to pay it because she never considered it hers in the first place. It was always the first thing she took care of, and somehow the money was always there to meet this obligation.

Twice a year she receives a letter from her boy in Burundi. It takes ten months for his letter to reach her, so in October she received a letter telling her that the Christmas money had been used to buy beans and paper.

47

"It's good for people to give," Sherrill says. "It helps us take our eyes off ourselves, our needs, our wants, and realize how much we have."

Her father, Glen, says he talks with many people who want to help meet the needs of the world but don't know how to go about it. Giving to needy children through the auspices of a reputable organization is a tangible way to make a tiny dent in the need.

He suggests that anyone interested in such a program first look into the finances of the organization. Pay attention particularly to administrative costs. In some organizations, 80 percent of what you give goes to pay staff salaries. Sherrill says the organization through which she gives sends 85 percent to the child.

You, too, will want to find an organization with low overhead that sends most of the money taken in to the children, rather than keeping it for administrative functions. It is possible to check an organization's financial information through the Evangelical Counsel for Financial Accountability (ECFA).

Teach Them to Care for What You Have

One of the best ways to save money is not to spend it, and one of the ways to avoid spending it needlessly is to take care of the possessions you have.

We've probably all been in homes where children were allowed to be unruly. They may jump on the beds and furniture, write on the walls, throw garbage in the yard, and leave food sitting about. Besides being just plain messy, such misuse of a home and furnishings is expensive.

Sofa and chairs that have been used for a springboard have to be replaced or at least reupholstered—both costly expenditures. Beds that have been used in the same way have to have new mattresses. Spilled food damages carpets and furnishings. It costs money to repaint walls.

We need to consider everything we have as a gift from God. He helps us work for money to buy the things we have, but we are only the caretakers of those things he has loaned us. When we have finished with this life, we leave our possessions behind. An old proverb says, "There are no pockets in a shroud."

Teach Them to Use and Reuse What You Have

On the cover of a recent *Yankee* magazine was a picture of a crewel-stitched sampler that read, "Use it up, wear it out, make it do, or do without." The entire issue was devoted to Yankee thrift. I found myself laughing with delight at some of the ways New Englanders have found to save money. I laughed because we had followed many of those same practices in my growing-up years in Montana.

Many homes in Montana boasted a shed, attic, or other storage area stuffed with odds and ends that truly should have been thrown out—hood ornaments, bicycle wheels, stacks of old magazines, coffee cans, woodstoves. "It might come in handy someday," we'd say, or, "When I collect enough (whatever), I'll take it to the salvage yard. Who knows? I might make five bucks."

I love this story of thrift by Donald Hall, from *Yankee* magazine.

My cousin Freeman Morrison, who died 30-some years ago, was the thriftiest man in the thriftiest county of the thriftiest state. He never threw anything away. When he ate shredded wheat, he saved the cardboard partitions because they fit into boot bottoms and he didn't need to buy a Cat's Paw at Newberry's. When Free shot his annual deer, he ate everything edible, used the hooves for weights on piles of picked-up newspaper, and tacked the skin over the boards of his shack to keep the wind out.

When Freeman wished to bathe himself and the ice was out of Eagle Pond, he waded into the water fully clothed with a bar of soap—he made the soap—and washed his clothes and himself at the same time. It's true, Free carried with him a characteristic effluence; even if your eyes were closed, you knew when Freeman walked into the room. (Maybe it kept blackflies off.) And what did Free gain, for all his frugality? Independence: He never worked for anybody's wages unless he wanted to. To live without requiring cash is the greatest freedom.[7]

Most of us cannot live without cash, but if we would learn to "use it up, wear it out, make it do, or do without," we'd have a lot more resources for family fun than we do now.

Beside our concern for being frugal with money, there is a growing concern for being frugal with the earth. Every day we hear more horror stories about the mounting piles of garbage we produce. We simply must find a way to cut down on our consumption of natural resources. Not only are we depleting our resources, we are also filling up the earth with garbage.

Babies once wore cloth diapers instead of today's disposable ones that are clogging our landfills. They can do it again. We don't have to have every item in our grocery bag wrapped in plastic before it's put in the paper sack; in fact, we don't even need the paper sack. Europeans have been doing without them for years.

I rather suspect that our children will be the ones to lead us out of this environmental morass. Through their school programs and television, they are being made aware of the delicate balance of nature on our planet. As a parent, you can start the process of teaching environmental concern by never letting your children throw a paper wrapper out the window of a car, never allowing them to drop a can or bottle along a trail, and by teaching them to always leave an area a little better than they found it. Teach them the wonder of nature and how to observe it. Buy them books that give them an appreciation for the marvels of creation God has given us.

Teach Them to Enjoy Possessions as Investments

If at all possible, try to own a few beautiful things as investments. Not only is this good business, but it teaches your children to appreciate the fine craftsmanship of previous generations, when things were made by hand. If you know the history of the objects, use them as history lessons to link your children with the past.

There is something about brushing your hand over an old rolltop desk from a long-ago lawyer's office that gives you a sense of the continuity of life. What kind of cases did he study here? What were the problems families brought to him to solve? What did he look like? Was he tall and skinny, short and fat? Was he old or young? Was he ever a daddy? What kind of a house did he live in? Where did this desk sit—in an office in his home, or in a storefront?

Teach your children to care for these lovely old possessions, but remember that you own them, they don't own you.

People Are More Important Than Things

People are more important than anything else on this earth. We must love people and use things, not the other way around. So while we teach children about budgets, investments, and ecology, we must remember that God gave us all of this for our use. He wants us to use it wisely, with appreciation and care, but we are not to love things. Things are not the most important part of life.

We need to move through life with an easy gratitude for what has been given us, and we need to keep a watchful eye on our attitude about our belongings. When we find ourselves yelling at our children because we're trying to protect some possession, we need to evaluate what's going on in our heads.

When we find all of our time wrapped up in caring for our possessions, we need to stop and take another look. What must be most important to us is other people and our relationships with one another. Things will be left behind at the end of our lives; relationships last for eternity.

Family Adventures for Little or No Money

- 🐾 Teach a child a craft—knitting, crocheting, simple woodcrafting, or gardening. This will enable the child to produce his own presents for Christmas and birthdays.
- 🐾 Help children make their own wrapping paper by block printing plain paper or paper bags with fruits

---

and vegetables cut in half. Potatoes can be carved into shapes; lemons and oranges make an interesting print; half of an apple will work, too.

🐦 Have your children help plan a vacation by sending for travel brochures and maps. Talk to them about how much money you have to spend each day, and enlist their ideas and help in stretching that money.

🐦 Encourage older children to have a garage sale. They should plan the day, do the advertising, collect the goods, mark the items, and plan what to do with unsold items. They should be allowed to keep any profits.

🐦 Let the children play store with your canned goods, using a muffin tin as a cash drawer. Provide small change or play money, and help them learn to make change and purchase wisely.

4

SU CASA, MI CASA

I have been seriously delayed while writing this book by an interesting series of events that gave me the grist for this chapter. It happened like this.

Three years ago we purchased a lovely Cape Cod home on the banks of Issaquah Creek in Washington State. I loved that house. It had one and one-half acres of lawn, fruit trees, two streams, and almost 3,000 square feet of space.

About a year after we bought the property, our property taxes took an alarming jump. Our mortgage payments rose from $1,200 a month, which had been a stretch with two incomes, to $1,800 a month. To top it all off, I completely wore out and decided to quit the job I had had for nine years.

It didn't take a genius to figure out that our days in that house were numbered. We stayed as long as possible, but finally the day came when we were totally out of money. I cried for a week, then wiped my eyes, called the realtor, put the house on the market, learned never again to fall in love with an investment, squared my shoulders, and looked forward.

Because things were so unsettled in our lives, we decided not to buy another house but to take up temporary residence in an apartment. By this time I had been interviewed for a position in another state. Soon I received an offer of a job as book editor in Colorado Springs.

I stood in the middle of the floor at the apartment, holding a packing box, talking to my new boss on the phone, and wondering what to do next—pack or unpack.

In a few weeks I flew to Colorado Springs to buy a house I had spotted in a real-estate magazine, a brand-new Cape Cod. Arriving in Colorado Springs, I discovered the house had been sold two days before. It was very disappointing. But at this very moment the house I loved is under construction.

So, I've been through the process of selling a house (dozens of papers to sign), living in two apartments (dealing with leases), buying land (more papers), and starting to build a new home (working with a contractor to set up a construction loan). If I'm not qualified to write about finding shelter now, I never will be qualified. It's been a great experience, and there's more to come as the house comes into being.

There are some things to be learned. Lesson number one is: Don't fall in love with your investments. Number two is: Don't buy more house and more things to go into that house than are really necessary to sustain life. We overbuy, causing ourselves financial stress. Stress is further increased because we have to take care of all that property and those possessions. It is easy to quickly get into the position of having our things own us rather than our owning them.

Lesson three is: One way to save money on housing is to move to an area of the country where the cost of housing is lower, as it is here in Colorado Springs. Moving to a new location may not be an option for many people, but it is something worth considering, not just for housing needs, but in terms of life-style, family interests, educational needs, cultural needs, and extended family needs.

Some families have never considered such a move, even when it might enhance their entire way of life. I'm not campaigning for people to move to Colorado Springs or anywhere else, but housing costs *are* low here in Colorado, and recreational opportunities abound. Also, the pace of life is slower here than it is in many places. Of course, you cannot consider changing locations unless you can find employment.

Lesson number four is: Life can be simplified, at least for a time, by moving into smaller quarters. Apartment or townhouse living has its good side. Someone else mows the lawn. Someone else drags the hoses. Someone else paints and fixes (a seemingly never-ending job). Someone else does the gardens. Gardening's the part I miss most, but that can be solved by container gardening on a deck or patio.

We are very spoiled here in the United States. We think we have to have single-family dwellings; it's a part of the American dream. But the truth is, most of the rest of the world lives in multiple-dwelling buildings, and they do very well. We need to accurately assess our needs and live accordingly.

My mother always had the philosophy that a child would not remember, nor would he care, if his parents owned the house he lived in. He would not remember if the carpet was worn or if the furniture was threadbare, but he would remember the fun times he had with his parents.

I remember a time when we were just children and Mom and Dad's philosophy was carried out in our behalf. We were on a camping vacation, probably because camping was inexpensive and there wasn't a lot of money to spare. On our way home, we went by a lake where speedboat rides were offered for a price—too high a price for our financial circumstances. We three children had never been in a fast powerboat like that one, so Dad talked the driver into giving us a shortened version of the ride for a shortened version of the fare. It was wonderful fun! We clung to the sides of the boat, our hair flying straight out behind us, spray soaking us to the skin, and we laughed and laughed.

This brings us back to the same concept we've emphasized again and again: priorities. Do you know what is truly important to your family? Are you providing for the important? Are you spending a portion of your income to build memories no one can ever take away from your children?

55

What Do We Need?

Only you can determine what your family truly needs in housing. Just remember those all-important priorities. If you buy a big new house in the most expensive part of town and your income is modest (assuming the bank would grant you a loan under such circumstances), you are going to have less income left for family fun.

Could you live in a simpler house with a lower monthly payment? When our family moved to Seattle, it was during a time of serious economic downturn for the city. In fact, there was a local joke about the imaginary billboard at the edge of town that said, "Will the last person out of Seattle please turn off the lights?"

We sold our rather simple house in California and had that money to put toward a down payment. By borrowing some additional money from my parents, we were able to pick up an existing mortgage at $5\frac{1}{4}$ percent. It seems unbelievable now. Anyway, the net result was that the monthly payments were only about $250 a month.

Our income wasn't all that great, but with a house payment as low as that, there was still a little left for family fun and recreation. Over the years we remodeled the house in a couple of stages. We made some major improvements such as double-glazed windows and extra insulation in the walls and under the floors. We pulled up the old shag carpets and had the hardwood floors refinished. We also added a big deck off the dining area, which was like adding another room. When it came time to sell the house, we sold it for four times what we had paid for it.

Could you do the same?

Do you really need a house right now? Could you live in an apartment permanently? If not, could you live in an apartment for a while and save toward a bigger down payment?

A bigger down payment means lower monthly payments. Some economists encourage us to make small down payments and use the bank's money as long as possible. Yet that larger monthly payment haunts you for the next thirty years. Your investment may grow rapidly over those thirty years, but your children will also grow rapidly during that time. By the time the big monthly payments end and the house is yours, it will probably be too big for you because your children will have grown and gone. If the house payment is always a stretch for your pocketbook, you probably will have little left for recreation during the next thirty years. On the other hand, a small monthly payment means more cash in the system for fun.

How Can We Know What We Need?

God works in wonderful ways, as he did when I came to Colorado Springs to look for a house. I saw a house I liked in one of those free real-estate magazines you pick up in a supermarket. The agent who had placed the ad had a toll-free telephone number, so I called her. I didn't know it then, but I had just discovered one of the sharpest real-estate agents in Colorado Springs— one who also loves God.

As soon as I contacted her office, Joyce's assistant sent me information. One of the things in the packet was a housing requirements checklist (see p. 58), which is a good way to begin assessing your family's needs for shelter.

What Do We Want?

Closely tied to the question of what we need is the question of what we want. This question is closely tied to your family's lifestyle.

Some questions to ask yourself are:

1. Do we really want to buy our own home?
2. Do we want to take care of the house payment, repairs, maintenance, gardens, and so forth?
3. Do we want a one-, two-, or three-story house? Why?
4. Do we want a house that accommodates visitors?
5. Do we want a wood, brick, or stucco house?
6. What style of house do we want: colonial, ranch, split-level, contemporary, ultramodern?

CONFIDENTIAL HOUSING REQUIREMENTS CHECKLIST

Begin your house-hunting process in the comfort of your easy chair. Complete this form and return it to us. The more information we have about you prior to the actual house-hunting trip, the more efficient we can be in meeting your needs. We will run a computer search of all current listings and send you specific information on those homes that meet your requirements.

Name _____ Home phone _____

Address _____ Work phone _____

_____

Number of adults in family _____ Spouse's name _____

Number of children _____ Boys, ages ____, ____ Girls, ages____, ____

School requirements: Public _____ Private _____ Parochial _____

Level: Day care _____ Kindergarten_____ Elementary_____Grades 7–8 _____

Grades 9–12 _____ University_____ Other _____

Special education requirements_____

Currently live in: Home _____ Apartment _____ Other_____

Current home on market: Yes ____ No ____ Approx. size_____ sq. ft.

List price of current home, if on market_____

Type home desired: New ____ Pre-owned, age____ Condo ____ Rental ____

Apartment ___

Expected approximate down payment _____

Preferred monthly payment, including taxes and insurance_____

Preferred financing: Conventional ____ FHA _____ VA _____ Other_____

Architectural style preferences _____

_____

Number of bedrooms _____ Number baths _____ Family room _____

Formal dining room _____ Formal living room _____

Breakfast area _____ Fireplace _____ Garage _____

Other _____

_____

_____

Maximum acceptable commuting time _____minutes

Presently employed in Colorado Springs: Yes _____ No _____

Employer_____

Office address _____

Special facilities you must be near _____

_____

House hunting trip planned for _____ to _____

Need hotel accomodation assistance? Yes_____ No_____

Will be staying at _____ Phone _____

Need airport pickup? Yes ____ No ____ Other arrangements you need_____

_____

Please send additional information on the following _____

_____

_____

Comments_____

_____

_____

_____

7. Do we want a garden? flower beds?

8. How much land do we want?

9. Do we want a place for animals? large animals such as horses and cows? small animals such as cats and dogs?

10. Do we want a play yard? a service yard?

11. Is a view important?

12. Do we want a house that is highly resellable?

13. What kind of neighborhood do we want?

14. Do we want to live near the water?

15. How far away from schools and shopping do we want to be?

16. How good is the school district?

17. Are there special programs for disabled children, gifted children, and others with special needs?

18. How far from freeways and main arterials do we want to be?

19. How many rooms do we need?

20. How many bedrooms do we need?

21. How long do we plan to live in the house?

At some point you will realize you can't have everything you want. You'll have to settle for getting the most you can for the money you have.

Can We Afford What We Want?

It's not enough to know exactly what we need and want; we must also be able to pay for the house of our dreams. After some young couples consider their wants and needs and then look at their finances, owning a house seems positively out of sight. But we Americans are a resourceful people, and somehow most of us eventually find a way to finance our dreams.

Here are some ideas for getting a home of your own:

1. Buy a Housing Utility District (HUD) house. In some areas, HUD houses are still available at very reasonable

59

prices. HUD houses come pretty much "as is," but if there is no structural damage and what is needed is remodeling and redecorating, these houses are great bargains. The house can be repaired, painted, fixed up, and either lived in at a reasonable rate or resold, giving you a chance to buy a better home.

2. Buy an older home. Some older homes are not only cheaper but closer to city centers, which may solve the family's transportation problems. Many of them are located on established public transit lines, eliminating the need for a second car. More dollars saved.

3. Accumulate a larger down payment. Since the trend now seems to be toward marrying later in life, many people are able to accumulate a nice savings account by the time they marry and need a home. If the amount you need to finance can be lowered by a larger down payment, you will probably be able to afford a larger, better home.

4. Buy a smaller house. Many years ago, when families were large, people had to have huge homes. Couples today are having fewer children, so they can get by with smaller houses.

I was recently on a house tour and visited a very small house that a young couple had remodeled. All the rooms were small, and there weren't very many of them, but the couple had used the same color scheme throughout the house, tying all the rooms together visually and giving the feeling of more space.

The house had been on the market for a long time before the couple bought it, because it was virtually a dump, but this couple had seen its potential and picked it up at a low price. The house's location was ideal, since it was on a waterway leading to a major lake—truly a prime location. They added a wing on one side, making the house "U" shaped. In the center of the U they installed a very nice, but small, swimming pool. The pool was their one big extravagance, but it was also the item that made the place special enough to be on a community house tour.

5. Consider two incomes. In many places, the only way a family can have its own home is to have two incomes. That either means one parent works two jobs or, more often, both parents work. If we find ourselves in this situation, we need to weigh carefully the importance of owning our own homes against not being there when our babies take their first steps and say their first words. You are the only one who can make that determination, and it needs to be made with much prayer and concern.

6. Watch the paper for foreclosure sales. In certain areas of the country, you may be able to find a real bargain in housing this way.

7. Find a builder who has overextended himself financially. It happens sometimes, and you'll not only help yourself, but you'll help the builder get out of his predicament. In this case you might have to roll up your sleeves and finish off several of the rooms. Can you do that? Do you have the skills? Can you live with the confusion and the mess?

8. Find a bargain by moving to the edge of the suburbs. Land may still be relatively inexpensive there.

9. Buy an "oddball" house. There are some real bargain houses, which have a poor arrangement of rooms, strange window placement, terrible paint or stonework, and all kinds of esthetic problems. These houses are great candidates for remodeling. Magazines are filled with stories of people who have done this. But you need to be very careful. Seek the services of structural engineers and architects before you buy such a place. In other words, know what you are doing and be sure you have the ability to restore the house before you buy it. Know, too, that while the initial outlay of money for a down payment may be small, you may sink everything you make into the house for the next fifteen years. Buyer beware!

61

10. Buy off-season. There are seasons for house buying, just as there are for most other commodities. January and February are great months for finding house bargains. So are July and August, when many people are on vacation.

    I understand why many people do not want to house hunt during the winter months. I always marveled at how different houses in the Northwest looked on a sunny day than they did on a typically overcast, dark January or February day. But it might be possible to find a real bargain on one of those dark days. Take advantage of the off-season for real estate.

11. Don't be afraid to make a low offer on a house. If you find something you like, make an offer that seems fair to you, even if it's well below the asking price. You never know. Be careful not to give away the fact that you've finally found what you want. Even though you love the house and feel you'll never find another so perfect for you, the truth is that there will be other houses that will work out just as well.

Other Kinds of Housing

There are a number of other kinds of housing that may be more affordable than a single-family dwelling. Let's take a quick look at some of these.

Co-op apartments or condominiums are one alternative to owning a single-family home. All kinds of people are moving into these units—singles, the aging, empty nesters, and full families. This type of housing is ideal for people who want to own their own home but don't want the responsibility of a lot of maintenance work.

When you own your own condominium, townhouse, or other kind of co-op apartment, you can paint, paper, and pound nails to your heart's content. The inside belongs to you.

When you buy into a co-op situation, you buy into a corporation that owns and runs the building. In addition to your monthly mortgage payment, you will pay a maintenance fee for care of the grounds and the exterior of the building.

As in most cases, this kind of housing has its advantages and disadvantages. The advantages have been stated. The disadvantages are that you will most likely have at least one common wall with your neighbors. You may hear some noise from them. You need to decide if that is a problem for you.

My friend Deb and her little girl Jamie are buying a townhouse. She thinks it's a great way to live. Although the payments are sometimes a stretch for her, they are building equity. Her townhouse happens to border a very large park where all kinds of summer and winter activities take place. Nearby is a community garden site where Deb and Jamie have had a garden for the last few years. It's a good housing solution for these two.

The apartment we're living in houses families with children and pets. Once in a while we hear the bassett hound who lives next door bark, and I sometimes hear the children in the hall. I, personally, find the sounds of nearby life very comforting, but you must decide what is comfortable for you. See what the housing rules are concerning pets, noise, children, and so forth and then decide if you can live with the situation.

Probably the biggest drawback to buying a condominium or other multiple dwelling is the resale value. These types of property do not escalate in value as much as single-family dwellings and may be more difficult to sell.

Another drawback can be the financial health of the developer. Check to see he or she is highly reputable, well financed, and experienced in the field. This is especially true of a new development.

The most affordable private housing is a mobile home. When you buy a mobile home, you get the complete package, and once set up, it is ready to be lived in.

There are fees to "park" the home in a mobile-home park. There are also installation fees, and some mobile parks specify that the homes must be set on concrete and have skirting and steps to the door. There will be plumbing and electrical hookup fees, as well.

Insurance for a mobile home is higher than for a comparably sized conventional house. Mobile homes often fall victim to fires and wind (tornado) damage, and this has caused insurance rates to skyrocket.

The greatest disadvantage to mobile homes is that instead of increasing in value like a conventional single-family dwelling, they tend to depreciate, like a car. Mobile homes may provide a quick remedy to a housing need, but one needs to think seriously about the loss of investment earnings with such a home.

Some people buy a piece of land and then install a used mobile home that has already taken the serious depreciation that happens in the first five years. This can give them an opportunity to begin living on their own land, working the land, and begin construction of a conventional home.

The other obvious problem with a mobile home is the lack of space and storage, both of which are in short supply.

Once again, only you can weigh the needs of your family and decide what is best in your situation. Perhaps mobile home living will give you the needed funds for family vacations and fun times. Perhaps living in a mobile home and building your permanent dream house together as a family would be a great way to build strength into your family life.

How to Buy a House

Buying a house is a rather complicated business, as you will see when you begin signing document after document after document. There are rules for everything, and they are all documented, and they all have to be signed.

Rather than attempting to explain the process here, let me encourage you to do some reading on the subject. Once again, a well-qualified real-estate agent will be a tremendous help in getting you into your house.

Talk early on with a banker and get started on credit checks. Try to plan your house buying to take advantage of low interest rates. You will save thousands and thousands of dollars over the life of your mortgage.

Look at your house as a wonderful place to rear your family, a possession in which you can take pride, and a great investment. In most places in the country, real estate still steadily increases in value.

After a house is purchased, there's a lot more to do to make it a home. A home means furnishings, appliances, entertainment equipment, rugs, curtains, pictures, dishes, pots and pans, ad infinitum. Later on, I'll share some of my ideas and secrets for making a house a home—inexpensively.

Family Adventures for Little or No Money

- If your library has art prints to check out, bring some home and hang them up. Try to find out something about the artists and the pictures.
- Use Styrofoam trays for picture frames or let the kids weave colorful scrap yarn back and forth across the trays to form designs. They can use a large, dull-pointed tapestry needle to punch through the edges of the tray.
- Make a pincushion. Using pinking shears, cut two layers of fabric or felt in a variety of shapes. Let the kids sew two layers together (make sure to leave an opening for stuffing). Stuff with old nylon stockings or polyester filling. Sew the opening shut and attach a loop of ribbon or yarn for a hanger.
- Make pictures by gluing various macaroni shapes to cardboard. Paint with acrylic paints.

5

PUT ANOTHER POTATO IN THE SOUP

"Isn't this wonderful? We've grown or provided everything on this table except the butter, the tea, and the sugar." If I've heard it once, I've heard it a thousand times. I heard it again just recently when visiting Mom and Dad.

I looked at the table and, sure enough, it was true. There was a green salad made from homegrown lettuce, dressed with green onions and tomatoes from Dad's greenhouse. There were snow-white, fluffy, baked potatoes and sweet carrots from his garden. There was home-canned fruit from Mom's pantry. On some occasions there might be bread, biscuits, or corn bread— all made from scratch. The jelly might well be made from chokecherries picked in the wild or red raspberries from Dad's carefully tended bushes. The meat often is wild game or trout. Both my parents are avid fishermen and hunters. (Before you get upset about that, let me say that they only take game for food, and they never waste it.)

When I was growing up, we often joked about being the "homemade" family. Basically everything we ate was either homegrown, harvested from the wild, bartered from neighbors, or purchased in bulk and then processed.

My folks really know how to make their food dollars stretch a long way. Breakfast cereal is often cracked wheat, old-fashioned oatmeal, or some other whole grain product. Have you any idea how inexpensive unprocessed grains are? And learning to eat them is easy.

Let's talk about not wasting food. On this score, I think my mother must be the world's thriftiest person. If something is left over, it is either served for lunch the following week or is resurrected in a new form for dinner.

When we were children, we used to groan when Mom made a huge turkey or a casserole dish that was overly large. We knew we'd end up eating it all—either now or later.

Every year that passes, it takes more and more money to put food on the family table. I am often appalled when the total is rung up at the grocery store and divided among my bags of groceries. Where once it averaged out to about $12 a bag, now it is more like $35 to $50, and sometimes I haven't even purchased meat or other protein products. What is a family to do?

Making Food Dollars Stretch

This is a very real problem, and if you need proof, just look at the magazines beside the checkout stands at the grocery store. You will always find one or two that tell you how you can feed your family on so many dollars per day (in a recent magazine, it was feeding a family of 4 for $84 a week); how to save big at the checkout; or yet one more plan for using coupons to save food dollars.

The bottom line of making food dollars stretch is having an attitude that says:

1. I'm going to make do with less-expensive products.
2. I'm going to honor my own wants and not be controlled by advertising.

3. I'm going to buy food value over food convenience.

4. I'm going to learn how to cook less-expensive cuts of meat in a way that makes them taste as good as the more-expensive cuts.

5. I'm going to realistically look at what I spend at the grocery store, determine how much is food and how much is nonfood products, and see if the nonfood items could be purchased more cheaply at another place.

6. I'm going to plan my menus before I go to the store, to help me avoid impulse buying.

7. I'm going to fight my own personal battle with inflated food prices.

Food is the biggest item in your weekly budget, and there is no way you can get by without eating. You have to find a way to eat more economically without seriously lowering your quality of life. The challenge is to find a way to cut down your food costs without anyone in the family realizing you're saving money on food.

Sylvia Porter says you can reduce your food costs at least 10 percent by observing simple tips for careful, sensible shopping. You can slash your costs more than 20 percent merely by "trading down" to products that are just as nutritious as expensive "convenience" items.

The question always comes down to: Do you have more time or money? If you have more money than time, buy convenience; if you have more time than money, trade down to less-expensive, less-convenient products.

There is no way you can eat like a king if you are not earning a king's income. Food tastes and food budgets must be tailored to available income. Unfortunately, those at the lower end of the earning scale spend a greater percentage of their income on food than do their more affluent neighbors. For many low-income families with several children, food can take up to half of their earnings. For a family making a moderate wage, it can be 25 percent, while for those with a higher income, it is only 10 or even 5 percent of available income.

I have never existed at the king's end of the income spectrum, but I have had to make it on an income that was below the poverty level. At the time we were living in a rural community in California, where most of our friends and acquaintances had gardens, and some even had livestock.

I soon became an expert on 599 ways to cook zucchini squash, because we were given about a thousand pounds of it a year. And each spring, a farm family would give us a lamb. Now I'm not particularly fond of lamb. I did learn to enjoy lamb chops and leg of lamb, but to this day I detest lamb stew.

There were other gifts, as well, including grocery bags full of artichokes and more tomatoes than anyone knows what to do with. Once there was a gift of prime beef, and there were always peaches, pears, plums, apricots, persimmons, and even various kinds of nuts.

I made it my business to utilize every bit of food that was shared with us. I purchased a secondhand freezer and began to fill it with the summer surplus to help us through the winter months.

I figured out ways to use every bit of leftover food and disguise it so that no one knew he was eating reruns. I kept a stockpot in the refrigerator, where little bits and pieces of leftovers were tossed, along with water from cooking vegetables and meat juices. Then I would add some fresh vegetables and lots of herbs and make soup for Saturday night suppers. Each week the soup had a slightly different texture and flavor, but it was always delicious. Served with homemade corn bread or baking-powder biscuits hot from the oven, supper didn't taste like leftovers.

My friend Candy is a master at making money stretch, and her food dollars are no exception. I love to stop by her apartment, because it always smells so good. There is always something wonderful simmering in a pot. I've eaten some of her cooking, and it tastes just as good as it smells. I asked her for her secrets.

Candy decided to invest her limited funds in some herbs and try her hand at ethnic cooking. She bought the herbs a few packets at a time at an import store, where they are much less expensive than the fancy bottled kind that supermarkets sell.

Then she acquired a few good ethnic cookbooks and started trying things. She tells me that vegetarian recipes are the best, and that it is simple to add some kind of meat to a vegetarian recipe if you are not a vegetarian. The vegetarian cookbooks have the best information for seasoning foods with herbs.

Then she takes simple cuts of beef, pork, lamb, or poultry and spices them up. Cheaper, tougher cuts of meat can be marinated to tenderize them. Various kinds of cheese and other dairy products can provide needed protein in the diet.

She doesn't use much prepared food, because it is always higher in price. She also uses lots of whole grains in her cooking. Grains such as rice, bulgur, wheat, and corn all add substantial nutrition at an inexpensive price. Homemade muffins are a favorite of Candy's. They are easy to make and taste wonderful.

Candy says, "Use artistry in the kitchen. Cooking can satisfy a creative urge as much as songwriting or painting." She also encourages low-fat cooking. Low-fat foods are often cheaper and are certainly better for you. "Sometimes instead of buying some fattening food, I buy a bunch of fresh flowers to keep me from feeling deprived. One bunch of mixed flowers will make several little color-spot bouquets."

"One other thing I do," says Candy, "is to precut a larger portion of meat into smaller portions just the right size for one meal. Another thing I do is use a crockpot. You can dump the ingredients in and forget it. The crockpot tenderizes tough cuts of meat."

I thought about Candy and a couple of my other friends who are living on slim earnings when I read a line from Michael Weiss's *The Clustering of America*. The author recounts sociologist Russell Lyon's claim that class has less to do with money than with taste, knowledge, and perceptiveness.

Candy and my other friends are building a quality, classy life, and they're doing it without a lot of money.

Some Factors That Affect How Much You Spend

1. The amount of available income.
2. The age of your family members (teenagers have hollow arms and legs that need hourly filling).
3. How much and what kind of entertaining you do.
4. The kinds of foods you prefer.
5. Where you live.
6. Weather conditions.
7. Whether you grow or process any of your own food.
8. How much you eat out.
9. How important food is to you, as compared to other wants and needs.
10. Inflation.
11. Family traditions surrounding food and eating.

Free Food

If you don't have a lot of money for food, you have to use your head and think about how to make your food dollars stretch. It is amazing to me how much food is wasted in this country. In many parts of the country, wild berry vines droop with unpicked fruit.

Last summer I walked two blocks from the house with a couple of buckets and returned in about half an hour with enough blackberries to make twelve pints of jelly. In this area of the country, as in most areas, there are all kinds of wild berries to be picked.

In my native Montana, which has one of the shortest growing seasons in the country, there are wild chokecherries, wild raspberries, and marvelous huckleberries to be picked.

Everywhere there are abandoned fruit trees where you can glean apples, plums, pears, and all other kinds of fruit. You do have to trim the fruit, watching for worms and other pests, but some people pay high prices for fruit grown without insecticides.

I like what Issaquah, the little town I lived in for three years, has done with its landscaping. I walked up and down Gilman Boulevard, the main thoroughfare, many times before I realized it was lined with fruit-bearing trees and plants.

First came the gooseberries, hanging in ripened clusters, begging for someone to pick them. Then it was blueberry season. This year I noticed many town citizens had caught on and were out harvesting the fruit. (The city fathers encouraged the citizens to pick the fruit.) Then the apples, pears, and apricots were ready, and the grapevines clinging to a chain-link fence gave up a rich harvest of sweet grapes.

I was a little timid about joining the fruit pickers early in the season, but by the time the grapes were ready, I went down with my bag and brought home about ten pounds of wonderfully sweet grapes. Some we ate fresh, and some I turned into jelly.

There's probably some free food in your area. I remember a time in California when a major packing plant went on strike at the height of the pear harvest. We drove out to the plant to discover mountains of pears slowly turning into a brown mass that smelled like vinegar. Since we had been away when the strike began, we were not as fortunate as our friends who brought home boxes and boxes of perfect fruit that they canned for winter.

Gathering free food is time-consuming. As far as I am concerned, there is nothing more tedious than picking huckleberries. I couldn't be persuaded to do it, if it wasn't so wonderful to sit in the sunshine on a hillside and talk with others who are also picking. It's a kind of therapy that money cannot buy.

Food Warehouses

During lean years, I discovered food warehouses, the kind that sell canned goods at a discount because the label isn't right, there has been a slight overcook on the processing, something has been spilled on the canned goods and made a mess of the labels, or perhaps the case has been broken.

73

Manufacturers don't have the time or money to replace labels or repackage broken cases, so all the damaged goods are purchased by food warehouses and resold at greatly reduced prices.

It is important to inspect cans for damage, just as it is important to inspect cans in a regular food store. Don't buy cans with rusted tops or bulging sides. Report them to the store's owner.

If you have a question about the quality of a certain brand of food, you can always buy one can and take it home and try it before buying more. Or you can carry a can opener with you, purchase one can, take it outside, open it, and inspect or taste it for quality. If it passes, go back inside and stock up.

There's a milling company in the Seattle area that sells whole-grain products. Most of the milling is done on-site, so it's a dusty place. The milled grains are stored in large rubber garbage cans. You have to scoop and package your own grain products.

The store sells everything from steel-cut oatmeal to millet. They also have whole, unroasted, unsalted nuts, a full line of herbs, cornmeal and all kinds of flour, bulk raisins and other dried fruit, lentils, beans, and dried peas. They carry coffee in bulk, as well as carob and chocolate chips. Here is a place where your money buys so much that you can barely stagger out under the weight of twenty dollars worth of food.

I have also visited mills where grain is still being ground on old-fashioned millstones powered by water. Visiting such a place with your family will help them understand how early settlers managed to take care of one aspect of their food needs.

Other kinds of food warehouses have sprung up in recent years—giant food warehouses where you can buy in bulk. Usually there is a membership fee, and you must weigh the cost of the membership fee, the ability to buy only in bulk (which can sometimes present storage problems), the wide variety of food which simply begs to be purchased, and the actual savings. Most warehouses will give you a trial shopping trip before you purchase a membership.

I find that although the savings are substantial, when I'm shopping at such warehouses, I spend more than I had intended and then have to find a place to store the food. However, if time is a factor, it will be timesaving to buy in bulk. I have discovered some excellent products and bargains at these warehouses.

For example, one such warehouse sells frozen boneless, skinless chicken breasts, which have virtually become a staple at our house. They are low in cholesterol, easily stored in the freezer, and quickly cooked by thawing in the microwave. Then they can be fully cooked in the microwave in three minutes, or broiled or panfried in olive oil and seasonings in just minutes.

I have also discovered this warehouse's ground beef is extra lean and of excellent quality. It comes, however, only in fifteen-pound packages. On the day I buy ground beef, I take time to make hamburger patties, which I slip between pieces of waxed paper and package six to a package. I also package meal-sized packages for casseroles and tacos.

Growing Your Own

Not only can growing your own food save you money, but it can provide you with fresh, nutritious, tasty meals. As I mentioned at the beginning of this chapter, my dad's garden provided much of what our family ate while I was growing up. Dad still has a garden that is so beautiful people stop and lean over the fence to look at weedless rows of beans, peas, corn, chard, asparagus, potatoes, beets, carrots, raspberries, cabbage, and kohlrabies. A couple of years ago (and I do not exaggerate), Dad had a cabbage head that was two feet across, nestled down in a plant that was a good four feet across.

Putting By

If you enjoy gardening, and if you are willing to process the foods you grow, then growing your own food can be an excellent way to save money. There are many ways to process foods for long-term storage.

Canning

First let's talk about one old-fashioned way of putting by: canning. Canning involves quite a bit of work and equipment. You'll need canning jars, rings, and lids of various shapes and sizes. You'll need some kind of kettle or pressure cooker for processing. You'll need to pick, buy, and prepare the fruit and vegetables for canning. You'll need to prepare syrup for packing fruits, and brines for making pickles. And you'll also need a good book about canning and processing foods.

Home-canned foods, improperly processed, can be lethal, two of the worst being green beans and any kind of meat product. I remember that early in my homemaking career, I canned some green beans. While I was growing up, I had home-canned lots of green beans for my mother, so I knew it was important to be careful. But my mother had a pressure cooker, which kills any toxic bacteria, and I did not. I even consulted a canning book and thought I had done it properly.

One day I checked my canned stores and found the tops of the bean containers bulging. Needless to say, I couldn't throw them away quickly enough. In rechecking, I found that I had cooked the beans half as long as I should have.

That incident put cold dread in my heart. How easy it would be to make a serious mistake with home canning and end up with someone getting botulism poisoning. After that I stuck to highly acidic foods such as tomatoes and pickles and to fruits preserved in sugar syrups. All of these are relatively safe and much less complicated to prepare.

Dehydration

Dehydrating foods is fun and easy to do. All it requires is some means of dehydrating the food, and there are inexpensive countertop units for this.

Food must be sliced in thin wafers or strips and laid out on trays that are often made of fine nylon screening. The unit keeps an even temperature and provides air circulation. Within a couple of days, the food is dried out and can be packaged and stored in containers for long periods of time.

If you have a dehydrating unit, you can take advantage of supermarket sales of overripe fruit. Fruit has the most sugar when it is fully ripe, but it will not survive long on the store's shelves, so you can often find bananas for a few cents a pound and peaches and pears at the peak of ripeness.

These fruits are wonderful when sliced and dehydrated. They make great nutritious snacks, and the homemade variety is superior to the kind you can buy in health-food stores. Most fruit snacks in health-food stores have been treated to keep them from turning brown.

Other easy-to-do and delicious dried fruit snacks are apples, apricots, pineapple, and raisins.

I used to dry lots of green peppers and mushrooms when they were inexpensive. When making soups or casseroles, it was easy to toss in a handful for flavoring.

I've always grown my own herbs; I think it's the sign of a lazy gardener. Herbs thrive on neglect—my kind of gardening. Over-fertilized herbs lose a lot of their flavor.

Herbs are wonderful additions to food, and by using herbs in cookery, you can avoid overusing salt. Herbs can help you develop a reputation as a great cook, and they are extremely easy to dehydrate.

I have trouble growing basil. The slugs, snails, and bugs like it as much as I do. So each summer, I go to a farmers' market and buy two or three huge bunches of basil. Then I walk back to the car, drowning in its wonderful fragrance.

Once home, I wash and dry the basil, separate the large stems from the smaller ones, and spread them out to dehydrate. Thick pieces of stem take too long to dry. When the basil is thoroughly dry, I chop it up in the blender until it is reduced to powder; then I put it in tightly sealed jars and use it all winter.

The same goes for all the other herbs: oregano, chives, parsley, sage, rosemary, thyme, mint, and winter savory for eating. Scented geraniums and lavender are great for potpourris. When stirred together with dried rose petals and orris root, these make splendid-smelling concoctions to scent your home.

Get a good book on dehydrating food and a simple unit, and experiment. Just remember, when you are stuffing banana chips, pineapple bits, dried apricots, or homemade raisins into your mouth, you may have removed the water from the fresh

77

fruit, but you have not removed the calories. If you're counting calories, watch out!

Freezing

Freezing is probably the easiest of the "putting by" techniques. Owning a home freezer may be one of the best money-saving investments you can make.

When you own a freezer, you can not only freeze fruits and vegetables at the peak of their season, but you can also visit a bakery thrift store and stock up on breads, pies, cakes, and cookies, all of which can be frozen and are freshened by the freezing process. You can also buy a side of beef or a lot of chicken when the price drops, or just take advantage of meat specials at the supermarket each week.

There are all kinds of ideas about how to freeze food. Get a good book and follow the directions. When I lived among the farmers in California, they pooh-pooed the need to blanch fruits and vegetables in boiling water before freezing, so I tried freezing ears of corn that had only been cleaned and had not been blanched. I honestly could not tell the difference.

For a number of years I had some ever-bearing raspberry bushes. At the height of the season the berries had to be picked at least every other day, and I didn't have time to do much with them. I picked them as cleanly as I could and put them in containers that went straight into the freezer. Later I'd take them out and turn them into one of my favorite condiments, red raspberry jam.

Meats, fish, bakery goods, margarine and butter, fruits and vegetables, and even cheese (which crumbles after it has been frozen and is best used for cooking) can be frozen. Of course, if you own a freezer, it is possible to take advantage of frozen-food sales and stock up at great savings.

Perhaps "putting by" is one of the most comforting money-saving activities in which one can engage. A freezer stuffed full of good food, shelves lined with beautifully packed fruit, cupboards full of dehydrated herbs, fruits, and vegetables, a bin brimming over with potatoes, can give one a sense of great comfort and security.

Teaching your children how to provide for their needs through the process of "putting by" is a valuable lesson in thrift that will stand by them all through their lives.

When It Comes to Entertaining

I think entertaining others in your home is one of the finest activities for a family.

In the first place, it is a biblical concept: "thereby some have entertained angels unawares" (Hebrews 13:2 KJV). The idea of hospitality is found throughout the Bible. In the oriental culture of the Bible, the attitude toward hospitality was that once a guest entered your home, everything you had was his. It was as if he owned it, which is a bit further than most of us want to go.

Bringing others into your home can be a wonderful learning experience for your children. Your table can literally become the crossroads of the world. Colleges and universities are full of international students who would love to be invited to an American home, and there are some American kids who are away from home for the first time and would enjoy a home-cooked meal.

There are people who travel for a living who would be delighted to spend a night in a home instead of yet another hotel. There are business associates who would respond in a relaxed, positive way if they could share a meal at our tables. There are artists and musicians and storytellers who could bring delight and wonder to our children's lives. There are older people who feel life has gone on without them and they no longer have value to anyone. Entertaining others is a little bit of work, but the rewards far outweigh the labor.

Entertaining—which usually involves food in some way—can be as expensive or inexpensive as you make it. During the lean times of my life, our work necessitated a lot of entertaining. I love company, so I never got tired of cooking for these guests.

Early on I decided that anyone who dropped by the house just before or during dinner was welcome to join us at the table, but he had to eat whatever I was fixing. I never had anyone turn down the food being served.

Usually when I invited guests, I tried to make it a special time. Menus usually were a little more elaborate, but not always. I distinctly remember a time when a minister friend, who was conducting a seminar at our church, was with us for dinner. I don't remember why, but I served him stew. It was a good stew with lots of fresh vegetables, and I probably served some kind of homemade bread with it.

I remember how that man ate and how he enjoyed it. He commented that now that his children were grown, his wife hardly ever fixed stew, and he missed it.

Stew is not an expensive dish, but seasoned well, served with style and flair and with an air of hospitality that says, "You're welcome here, and I want to share what we have with you," it is a memorable meal.

If you can't afford a full meal, why not serve dessert and coffee? What about lunch or breakfast? What about a popcorn and video night for teenagers? or a cookie bake-off for younger kids who are allowed to eat all the cookies they want?

Another way to entertain with style is to serve ethnic food. Many ethnic cultures feature inexpensive food. Spaghetti or lasagna, served with a big tossed salad and bread sticks on a red-and-white-checked cloth by candlelight, can be as much fun as a crown roast of pork dinner.

It has been my experience that when the atmosphere of a home shouts, "You're welcome here," people almost forget what they are eating. I guess if it were terrible food, they would notice, but what you serve may not be as important as how you serve it.

Just a word about table settings. Good food in good company served on paper plates will be enjoyed, but it is also possible to acquire flatware, dishes, glassware, tablecloths, napkins, and all the other niceties rather inexpensively. Most of these things can be acquired through garage sales, import stores, estate sales, and department-store closeouts.

I got rid of a complete set of china that I had stopped using, because for the last few years I have been acquiring, piece by piece, red and white pottery from England. Very few pieces of my dinnerware match, and yet when the table is set with this mixed red-and-white pottery, the effect is charming and provides interesting table talk.

Some of the pieces I acquired at the Wedgwood factory in England, others at a shop next to Westminster Abbey, and still others in open-air markets in England. I've also purchased pieces at antique shows and flea markets here in the United States, but most of it has come one piece at a time from thrift shops all over the country.

I could afford to go and buy a matched set of red-and-white pottery from England, but it is a whole lot more fun the way I am doing it, and it provides a lot more interest to my guests. Sometimes I think I must have all of the patterns in red and white that were ever made; then I'll discover another and another. I enjoy these dishes so much that they are always on display in an open-front antique hutch.

When it is necessary to count the cost of entertaining guests, remember to keep it simple and do it with style. It may be nice to have a formal bouquet on the table, but it is less expensive to use cut flowers, decorative grasses, colored leaves, or pine boughs from your garden, which have been arranged informally. Such simple table arrangements were made popular by Jacqueline Kennedy when she was First Lady of the land. If it's good enough for the White House, it's good enough for my house.

A friend told me that she uses lots of candles when entertaining. She said low lights and candlelight add a wonderful charm and can hide all kinds of things, such as shabby carpet or less-than-perfect furniture.

A fire in the fireplace is an inviting focal point. Lately I've been inviting friends to come for lunch and for evening coffee. I like to spread it out in front of the fire in the living room. I cover a little tea table with a white cloth, add a candle and maybe a tiny bouquet of flowers, and we sit, talking the afternoon away. It's very pleasant.

Successful entertaining is as simple as creating and communicating an attitude that says, "I'm glad you've come to see me. I want this to be a special time for us to remember, because you're very important to me. Though what I have may be simple, and I may not have very much, I'll share what I have with you because you are my friend."

Ideas for Saving Food Dollars

1. Eliminate one slice of bread from your diet each day. You can pare six pounds from your figure in a year and save dollars.

2. Always use a shopping list. Buy only what you need, but be sure to buy everything you need for a particular dish. That way you will not have to go back for more ingredients. Every trip to the supermarket causes you to spend added food dollars. How many times have you gone for one item and come out with a bag full of food?

3. Buy eggs. If your cholesterol level can stand it, eggs are a good source of protein and are usually cheap.

4. Buy the least-expensive kind of cheddar cheese for cooking. Buy a better cheese for snacking.

5. Buy herbs in bags at import stores. Buy one each week until you have developed a good library of spices.

6. Plan your leftovers when you plan your menus. Sometimes you will not want any leftovers, sometimes you will. Slice beef from a large roast for sandwiches, chunks of beef from the same roast for stew.

7. Use skim milk for cooking. It's better for you and cheaper than reconstituted dry milk.

8. Shop without the kids. They can sabotage your food budget.

9. Don't shop when you are tired or hungry or when the store is crowded. You don't think through your purchases when you are in that state of mind.

10. Use coupons, but be careful not to buy more expensive items just because you have a coupon. Think it through before buying.

11. Buy generic or store brands. If you have a question as to their quality, buy one and try it. If it meets your standard, stock up on the next trip.

12. Buy "raw" food whenever possible. Remember that every time someone does something to your food, it adds to the cost. Besides that, you don't know what they have added to your food. Prepackaged, precooked, pre-breaded, pre-anything adds dollars to your food bill.

13. Pancakes made from a dry mix are cheaper than frozen pancakes and cheaper than a ready-pour mix.

14. Buy seasonal fruits and vegetables. Not only are they less expensive, they also taste better when they are at the peak of the season. Melons picked in midsummer always taste better than the first ones that appear in supermarkets in the spring.

15. Make your own trail mixes for snacking by mixing raisins, chocolate chips, peanuts, and your kids' favorite cereal. Put snack-size servings in plastic storage bags.

16. Remember that extra packaging raises prices. Buy huge bags of potato chips and repackage in smaller plastic bags. (They freeze well.) Buy a large container of instant oatmeal, rather than the small packets.

17. Buy cheese in bulk and spend a few minutes shredding it for topping casseroles and other dishes. Package in the amount needed for one dish. Cheese can be frozen if used for cooking.

18. Buy potatoes, carrots, onions, and grapefruit in large sacks. They are considerably cheaper than the individual items.

19. When buying a turkey, pick a large one. You get more meat per pound on a bird weighing twelve or more pounds.

20. Grind your own coffee at the store and save, but stay away from gourmet coffee beans if you are saving money.

21. Buy raisins in two-pound bags and repackage for snacks.

22. Buy boneless meat cuts whenever possible. Pound for pound, they're cheaper.

23. Sugared cereals are more expensive by far. They're not all that good for kids' teeth, either, but if sugar is not a consideration, then buy the unsugared variety and let them sweeten it from the sugar bowl for savings.

24. If possible, teach your kids to eat whole-grain cereals such as oatmeal and other cooked grains. The nutrition is excellent, and the savings are great.

25. Mix your own salad dressings from package mixes. You'll save significantly over bottled dressings.

26. When fruits and vegetables are at their peak, think about freezing some for use later on. Broccoli is very cheap at certain times of year. All you need to do is wash it thoroughly, blanch it in hot water for a couple of minutes, cool it under cold running water, and package it for the freezer.

27. Vegetables frozen in butter and those with other added seasonings and ingredients are nearly twice the price of the plain ones. By adding your own butter and herbs, you can save big.

28. Nothing could be easier to make than the new muffin mixes, and they are cheap. Buy them instead of fresh muffins from the bakery counter.

29. Use up leftover meat and poultry by grinding it with onions, a dash of Worcestershire, mustard and mayonnaise, for a hearty sandwich spread.

30. Sliver pork, chicken, or beef leftovers and stir-fry with fresh vegetables.

31. Crumble meat loaf and add it to spaghetti sauce.

32. Bits and pieces of ham or turkey can be added to an ordinary salad, to turn it into a great chef's salad.

33. Sliver cold leftover roast beef and serve it with a side dish. Hot Chinese mustard and sesame seeds make it special.

34. Keep a stockpot, or marinate bits and pieces of leftover vegetables and add to a salad.

35. Add cooked leftover vegetables to omelets.

36. Mash up the inside of leftover baked potatoes with a little milk until fluffy. Pile the potato back into the skin, top with cheese, bacon bits, onions, and reheat in the microwave.

37. Cook sliced onion in butter or margarine until just tender. Then add sliced leftover potatoes. Heat through thoroughly. Add shredded cheese, put a lid on the pan, and remove it from the heat. In a few minutes the cheese will be melted into the potatoes.

38. Serve leftover spaghetti cold as an oriental salad. Use a little soy sauce for seasoning, and add some sesame seeds.

39. Make croutons from dry bread.

40. Turn dry bread into crumbs by chopping it in the blender. These are great browned in butter and sprinkled over vegetables.

41. Make an elegant English trifle using leftover cake— preferably pound cake or angel food. Layer cake with peaches or raspberries, custard pudding, whipped cream, and toasted almonds.

42. Eat popcorn instead of chips. It's much cheaper and better for you.

43. Teach your kids to make cinnamon toast instead of filling up on cupcakes and other filled pastries.

44. Learn to eat simple desserts such as fruit and cookies, puddings, and frozen yogurt, rather than more expensive pies and cakes.

45. Buy and freeze day-old bakery goods if your family uses lots of them and can consume them quickly.

46. Use old-fashioned rice that has to be cooked twenty minutes, rather than instant rice that takes five minutes and costs twice as much. You can probably afford the extra fifteen minutes.

47. Check different forms of food—fresh, frozen, canned—to see which is the best buy. Do not assume one form is always cheaper than another.

48. Limit purchases of perishable foods, even when they are a great bargain. You are not saving money if the excess has to be thrown out.

49. Buy food in large containers if your family can consume it before it spoils. It is considerably cheaper (and more environmentally sound) than several small containers.

50. Select cuts and types of meat, poultry, and fish that provide the most cooked lean meat for the money spent. Some of the less-expensive cuts can also be the most flavorful, but must be prepared properly to tenderize them.

51. Serve less meat and mix it with vegetables, pastas, rice, and breads to make a little go farther.

52. Remove the fat from meat drippings and use the rest of the juices to flavor gravies, soups, and sauces.

53. Prepare meatless meals a couple times a week. Use beans, dry peas, and peanut butter as a protein source on those days.

Family Adventures for Little or No Money

- Go pick something found in the wild—apples, flowers (make sure they are not endangered species), strawberries, asparagus, or blueberries.
- Let little kids play in the kitchen sink with soap bubbles, an egg beater, and other cooking implements. When they've finished, simply wipe up.

6

VOGUE, GQ, AND OTHER EXPENSIVE MYTHS

I've always considered it a challenge to look as great as I can and spend as little money as possible. It's a game for me, and I've become quite skilled at it.

A standard line I hear from my friends is, "That's a beautiful outfit. Where did you get it?" When I smile slyly, they say, "Don't tell me how little you paid. I don't want to hear."

One day a friend and I were discussing an outfit I was wearing that happened to be made up of bits and pieces I had picked up over a number of years in a number of places. Finally she threw her head back and laughed. "You look like you stepped out of the pages of *Vogue* magazine, and when I add you up, you total about ten dollars. How do you do it?"

Well, I'm not going to tell all my secrets here, but I am going to share some of the principles I've learned to make clothing dollars stretch for every member of the family.

Buy Quality

If you buy a marvelous trendy suit for a very inexpensive price, but it starts to bag where you sit and the seams split out after you've worn it only a couple of times, you haven't really bought a bargain. By the time you replace your bargain garment, you may have spent more than if you'd bought a more expensive, better-quality suit in the first place.

Think in terms of investing in clothing. If you buy a three-hundred-dollar suit and wear it five years, that's only sixty dollars a year. It's possible to wear a classically styled, well-made garment even longer. I have a number of suits and dresses I've had for more than five years.

But there is a problem. With so many clothing options available, how do you find quality products? What is quality, anyway? There are some things you can look for. Here are some tips to help you determine top-caliber clothing.

Check the tag for fiber content. Natural fibers are always winners in the quality category, because they breathe. One-hundred-percent woolen garments can't be beaten for wearability, packability, and for holding their shape, especially if they are lined. One-hundred-percent-cotton garments need a lot of care to keep them looking their best (they wrinkle), but they *are* comfortable, and many quality garments are made of cotton. Some now have an easy-care finish to help them shed wrinkles. Linen is a quality fabric that wrinkles badly, especially when it is new. Repeated washing or cleaning softens linen. It seems, however, to be fashionable to be wrinkled when wearing a quality linen garment. Although silk is still considered a luxury fabric, it is much more available now than it was a few years ago.

Sewn into the garment somewhere you will find a care label. Look for it and determine if this garment is going to spend more time at the cleaner's than it does in your closet. Since we are talking about saving money for family fun, think twice about purchasing a garment that requires expensive dry cleaning.

There are all kinds of synthetic-blend fabrics. All have the advantage of easy care, but each has its own set of disadvantages, as well. One synthetic fabric that is very popular right now is rayon. Rayon gives colors a brightness and intensity that is delightful. It's inexpensive, but must be dry cleaned, and it also wrinkles unmercifully. It is not the fabric of high-quality garments.

Check seam allowances. Skimpy seam allowances or those that are frayed or puckered are the mark of inferior construction. Clothing with these problems will not last long in the washer and dryer, and they never look right.

On permanently pressed clothing, seams, hems, and the creases are also permanently pressed. You won't be able to let out a seam or lower a hemline on these garments without it showing. You can, of course, take in a seam or shorten a hem.

Check the zipper. It should lie flat. There should be no puckers around it. The teeth of the zipper should be painted to match the zipper tape. The weight of the zipper should be right for the type of fabric. If too lightweight, a zipper will break quickly.

Check the hem. Has a good quality hem tape been used? If it is loosely woven, it will come apart after a few washings or cleanings. Hems should have a deep allowance.

Check the lining. Is it of a good quality and color to match the exterior of the garment? Is it skimpy? Is it firmly attached to the garment in such a way that it doesn't hang down at the cuff or the bottom of the garment? Well-made dresses and pants are usually lined. A lining makes the garment hang better, increases durability, and decreases wrinkling and bagging.

Check the buttons. Perhaps nothing gives away the quality of a garment as quickly as its buttons. Buttons are the jewelry of the garment. Better-quality garments have beautiful buttons, and manufacturers usually provide one or two extra buttons in case you lose one. Good buttons are expensive, especially if you have to replace an entire set, so look for the extras and keep them handy.

Check the buttonholes. Bound buttonholes used to be the mark of quality clothing but are seldom seen anymore, even on the finest of clothing. The machine work on machine-made buttonholes should be tight and even, and there should be no threads hanging loose. Thread color should match the garment's color.

Check lapels. Lapels should be crisp and rolled slightly to the underside in a quality garment. If the lapel is limp when you first see it, don't buy the garment. Limpness happens quickly enough after you take the garment home. Also check to see if the upper lapel fabric is bonded to an interfacing. Sometimes these begin to separate in a bubbly pattern after one or two washings. It is sometimes difficult to determine if the top surface has been bonded to an iron-on interfacing.

Check underarm seams. Do they meet exactly? In mass-produced garments, the sleeves are sewn in before the side seams are closed, and sometimes the seams do not match. While this may not matter much to the look of the finished garment, it is an indication of shoddy workmanship.

Check all other seams. Puckered seams tell you the thread tension of one or both threads was set wrong, and is an indication of haste. Sometimes material may be caught in the stitches, causing puckering. At other times, the garment has been improperly pressed during construction and darts and pleats are lying the wrong way for a smooth fit.

Check belt eyelets. Are they smooth and finished so they won't tear out after one or two wearings? Is the belt washable on a washable garment? Is it dry cleanable on a dry cleanable garment?

Check pattern match. Plaids, stripes, tattersalls, and windowpane checked patterns should all match. Check where the sleeve and jacket are joined. Plaids and patterns should meet here, as well. Misaligned patterns shout "sloppy sewing."

Perhaps nothing will make you feel as good about yourself as wearing a well-made garment. It has been reported that Queen Elizabeth II of England told her heir, Prince Charles, "Clothes are important to a person of high rank." It's not entirely true that clothes make the man or woman, but it is true that clean, stylish, comfortable clothing will make you look better, and while we may not consider ourselves persons of high rank, we truly are important people and deserve to feel good about ourselves. When you are wearing quality clothing, you are able to forget about the clothes and concentrate on other people and things.

90

Sewing to Have More Clothes

Home sewing has never been as exciting or rewarding. There are beautiful fabrics from which to choose, designer patterns, gorgeous trim, and buttons. Knits are easy to sew, functional, and inexpensive. Serger sewing machines make the sewing of knits a snap.

If you have the time, you can sew almost any garment for yourself or your family and have it come out better than store-bought clothing. Sewing, however, is time-consuming, and you will have to determine if you are truly saving all that much by doing it.

It is wise to learn how to sew simple things, like a skirt. Well-made skirts can cost up to $125; you can make the same skirt out of the same fabric for around $25. Another big home-sewing saving is children's clothing. Children prefer simple clothing without a lot of fussy ruffles and trim. These can be easily constructed by the home sewer. If you can learn to make simple T-shirts for your children (a thirty-minute job), you can save a bundle, particularly if you watch for remnant pieces.

Every fabric store in the country offers instruction in making garments for both adults and children, accessory items, home decor projects, and crafts. The classes are usually free or are offered at a minimal fee. Often instructors give out coupons redeemable in fabrics and supplies. It's a great bargain.

Mending to Have More Clothes

My mother used to tell me repeatedly that if I would mend my clothes, I would have a lot more to wear. As a teenager that wasn't something I wanted to hear, but once in a while I would take her advice and mend ripped seams, put back hems that had come loose, and sew on buttons and trim. She was right. When I mended, I did have more to wear, and I also had less frustration, because when I wanted to wear something, it was ready. I didn't get all dressed and then look in the mirror only to discover my hem hanging loose.

91

You can fix clothing even if you don't sew. Hems, facings, interfacings, trims, and appliques all come as iron-on fusibles. There's a stick-and-sew zipper that will still require sewing, but at least it doesn't require pins and basting. The coated tape can be stuck and restuck to fabric without spotting the fabric. There are button replacement devices that don't require a needle.

Simple fix-its such as changing buttons, re-embroidering buttonholes to get rid of frayed edges, repairing torn belt loops, replacing seam and hem tapes, and repairing puckered seams all quickly upgrade a garment.

If even these simple tasks seem overwhelming, find a seamstress to help. A good seamstress should be able to repair a large number of garments in a couple of hours, as most repairs are minor. Repairing three-corner tears and replacing frayed collars and cuffs are not easy, but still may be worth the cost if the garment is of high quality. Quality clothing is worth the time and money it takes to keep it in good repair. In the long run, you'll be saving money.

Restyling: Not as Hard as You Think

One of the ways to extend your family's wardrobe is to remodel or restyle well-made clothing. This isn't as difficult as it may sound.

I have a navy blue linen blazer that I made nine years ago. This year military braid and trim are all the rage. So when I was visiting Cabrillo lighthouse in Southern California, I bought a replica set of lighthouse keeper's brass buttons. I will replace the plain dark blue buttons with these brass ones and add some gold military braid. I'll have an up-to-the-minute, high-fashion garment of excellent quality. It also will carry a bit of history and nostalgia because of the buttons.

Here are some other ways to restyle clothing:

1. Hems are shorter this year. Shorten skirts and dresses, but make sure they are still flattering to you.
2. Add trim and braid to plain clothing for a change.

3. Add fringe to a short skirt to add length and an entirely new look.

4. Use an oblong scarf as a belt with skirts, pants, and even shorts.

5. Hot glue appliques, shells, beads, feathers, and so forth to most anything—shirt fronts, hats, purses, shoes.

6. Change the buttons on a garment for instant pizzazz. There are even button covers that slip right over the existing buttons. I recently saw a trendy garment with every one of the seven front buttons different from the others.

7. Take the skirt or the jacket of a suit and pair it with lots of other tops and pants.

8. Use fusible materials to help with hemming, holding a facing in place, or attaching trim to a garment.

9. Take in or let out garments (unless they're permanent press) to get the best fit.

10. Don't buy a skirt that is too small around the waist. There usually isn't enough fabric to let it out.

11. Men's pants can usually be altered an inch or so larger or smaller. It is not a terribly difficult job to do.

12. Cut off children's jeans and pants for summer. You don't even need to hem them, as kids prefer them ragged.

13. Cut the long sleeves of sweatshirts and shirts off for summer. You might want to finish the shirtsleeves.

14. Restyle jackets and coats by sewing decorative patches on them. Kids love them.

15. Girls can use big brother's outgrown colored T-shirts for layering with their own shirts. Let them paint designs on the front.

16. Don't buy a garment with a gaping neckline or drooping shoulders unless you want that look. These mean that the garment is too big, and it will be impossible to correct.

17. Don't plan to lengthen a pleated skirt unless it is of wool flannel. The crease line will show permanently.

18. Don't buy a garment where the dart has been clipped or trimmed and plan to let it out. You can't.

19. It may be impossible to alter leathers and suedes and crisp fabrics such as taffeta, because the machine stitching may leave tiny pinholes.

20. Add thin cording to the edges of collars and lapels to trim them.

Accessorizing for Maximum Mileage

I have always been an accessory addict, and probably still have most of the accessory items I have acquired in the last fifteen years. I just keep recycling them for a new look.

I also have always been an advocate of buying the simplest, well-made garments and then giving them a new look every time I wear them through my choice of accessories.

The possibilities are endless, but here are some ideas to start you thinking:

1. Children's clothing needs little, if any, accessorizing. Accessory items just get in their way when they are playing. But book bags, hats, mittens, gloves, and scarves add interest and color. You will be replacing these items often, because children lose them constantly. Don't spend much money on them.

2. Ladies, use an oblong silk scarf tied in a perky bow for a belt.

3. Buy felt tams in a number of colors to vary the look of your own and your children's wardrobes.

4. Decorate those tams with pierced earrings. Just fasten them through the hat at the angle for a jaunty turn.

5. Use an antique pin, a scarf, silk flowers, ribbons, or feathers to decorate the brim of a hat.

6. Dress up plain pumps with shoe clips.

7. You can also use a shoe clip as a scarf holder. Just make sure the teeth on the clip will not damage the scarf.

8. Watch closeout sales for textured, patterned hosiery. Buy decorative winter weights during summer, when they are on sale. Winter will come again.

9. Collect silk scarves. They can be used in many ways; one of the best is at the neckline, where they draw attention to your face and add interest to plain garments.

10. Get a booklet that tells how to tie scarves for maximum effect.

11. Watch for sales on brightly colored, inexpensive costume jewelry. It adds interest and fun to your clothing.

12. Gloves are making a comeback as a fashion accessory. Buy them off-season, on sale.

13. Men's clothing can be updated and brightened by adding a new shirt, and a new silk tie and matching handkerchief.

14. Shoes that are properly cared for help give a man's wardrobe the finished look.

15. A well-made umbrella or briefcase also helps add the finishing touch to a man's wardrobe.

16. Men can add a vest or sweater for warmth and additional interest.

17. Both men and women can tie a sweater around their necks to give a jaunty look and also to have it available in case of chilly weather.

18. Shawls add dramatic interest to very plain dresses and suits. They can even be worn over coats for interest and added warmth. Small people have to be careful not to hide themselves in a shawl.

19. Don't forget your eyeglasses. They are an important accessory for both men and women. There is a trend toward having several pair of glasses for different occasions.

20. Sunglasses are an important accessory, too. Choose those that flatter your face. Avoid the reflective kinds that make

you look like a grasshopper or a helicopter pilot flying into the sun.

21. Pretty shades of hosiery show attention to detail and finish off an outfit. Carry an extra pair of stockings with you when you don't want to be seen with a run.

22. Don't overdo accessories. You can make yourself look like a Christmas tree.

23. Keep the rule of simple, elegant, and orderly dressing and accessorizing.

24. Have systems and cases for storing accessory items so that you don't have to search for the items when you are in a hurry.

Outlet Shopping

I read once that a true factory outlet is a room attached to the factory itself, like the Pendleton factory outlet in Washougel, Washington. There, in a portable building just across from the main entrance to the woolen factory, this famous company sells its goods at huge discounts. Some of the items are overruns on orders, some are seconds, but there often doesn't seem to be any reason why other garments are there. In addition to ready-made clothing, it is also possible to buy fabric, trim, buttons, and all the other sundries that go into making a Pendleton garment. If you can sew, you can make wonderful garments from Pendleton components at tremendous savings.

This outlet is a lot different from the outlet centers springing up all over the country. True outlets tend to have better prices on their goods, because the factories are very eager to sell old stock. A true factory outlet is owned by the manufacturer and sells only goods made in its factories, although there may be many labels on the goods.

At the Towle factory outlet in Massachusetts, I once bought silverplate for about one-fourth the retail cost. At other true outlets in that Massachusetts area, I bought skirts I'm still wearing after nine years, lingerie, and hosiery. All these purchases were made at tremendous savings.

All over the country, outlet malls are springing up; they have become a six-billion-dollar-a-year moneymaker.

I truly enjoy shopping at outlet centers. For one thing, everything I could possibly want to buy is in one place—everything from pots and pans to books, from designer clothes to toys. Besides that, there is usually a fun restaurant where you can get pizza by the slice, espresso, and marvelous desserts, among other wonderful edibles.

An outlet center is a great place for a family excursion. Besides being able to shop for everything you need and doing it together as a family, you can save from 30 to 70 percent.

If you are wondering where such outlets might be in your area, you can order two outlet guides. One is "The Joy of Outlet Shopping" and is available from Terry Dunhan, JOY Book, Box 7867, St. Petersburg, FL 33734. Price is $4.95. Another is "Outlet-bound, a Guide to the Nation's Best Outlets." Send to Outlet-bound, Box 12550WS, Orange, CT 06477. Price is $5.95.

Check your local bookstore and even the Chamber of Commerce in your area or in any area you will be visiting. My first introduction to outlet shopping came when we stopped at an information booth at the Massachusetts state line and were handed an outlet guide.

Here is some of the terminology that will help you be successful at outlet shopping:

Irregular—Items so marked will have slight imperfections that do not affect wearability.

Samples—Items made to show prospective buyers. They usually come in small sizes and often do not match other items in the designer's line.

"As is"—These are real markdown bargains, but be advised that there is always something wrong with these items. Check to find out what it is. It could be a broken zipper, soil, grease from manufacturing, or rips in the fabric itself. Find the flaw and decide if it is fixable or if it is a flaw you can live with for the price.

Discontinued—This means the line has been discontinued. You will not be able to replace or add to it later. This is probably more applicable to dishes and silverware than to clothing.

In addition to outlets, there are some other kinds of stores. They are:

Off-price stores that sell overruns and leftover goods from a variety of manufacturers rather than just one.

Discount stores that sell goods at a lower margin of profit than regular department stores.

Clearance centers that sell unsold seasonal goods from department store chains and other retailers.

To have the most success at shopping outlets, prepare ahead:

1. Go to local department stores and find out what the full prices of the goods are, for easy comparison.
2. Make a list of what you need. The selection can be overwhelming, once you reach the center.
3. Find out about store policies regarding credit cards, returns, and replacement of damaged goods.
4. Remember the only true bargain is the one you need. No matter how great the saving, if you don't need it, you aren't saving anything.
5. Check all clothing carefully for manufacturing defects. If you find them, ask for a higher discount.
6. Get your name on the store's mailing list.
7. Don't always believe the sizing marked in the garments. Sometimes the reason the garment is in an outlet center is because it was improperly sized.
8. Check the bins of jumbled, mixed items. Items here may be dirty or in other ways shopworn and only need washing or minor repair to bring them up to quality.

9. Think ahead. The clothing available in outlets may not be for the current season. Spring manufacturers' samples may come back for resale in the fall. If it is quality merchandise and of classic styling, it will still be in style next spring.

10. Take children only if they will enjoy the excursion and only if they can last a marathon shopping day. Most younger ones can't. Older children will enjoy the day most if the shopping is for them.

Thrifting

There is a way to save even more money than you can by shopping at outlets, discount, and close-out stores: Become a "junk store junkie." Shop at thrift and resale shops.

I am continually amazed at the amount and quality of goods that are thrown away in this country. Fortunately not all of it ends up in landfills right away. Sometimes several people have the opportunity to reuse an item before it is tossed for good.

I doubt if thrift-store shopping would be as good in less-prosperous countries of the world, but in this country, our affluence makes it possible for us to toss out items with scarcely a thought. Thrift-store operation is big business, and usually thrift stores are crammed with bargain hunters.

Thrifting is not for everyone. Some people just can't stand the process of sorting through lots of unusable, broken stuff to find that one treasure. But if you can do it, you can save a lot.

I've made thrifting a game—a very profitable one, at that. The thrift shop where I go most often buys overruns and returned merchandise from one of the more prestigious store chains in America. This company is known for its return policy and customer service. They will exchange or take back goods with no questions asked. A lot of that superior merchandise finds its way to this thrift-shop chain, where I buy it for about one-third of its original cost.

The chain also buys closeouts of stores that are shutting down, overruns, and "as is" items from local factories, salesmen's samples, and other new (tagged) items.

99

When I knew I would be writing this book, I started saving tags from the items I bought at this thrift-shop chain and marking on the back what had been purchased. Let me give you some ideas of the clothing I have purchased and the savings I have realized.

A two-piece red cotton dress with lined skirt—$12.99. (I bought this outfit in the dead of winter.)

A navy blue leather purse—fully lined in leather—with a shoulder strap—$5.99.

A two-piece cotton knit Lands' End dress—$6.99.

A red stitched-pleat skirt—$2.50. (This was on sale at half price. Even thrift stores have sales.)

A turquoise silk shell—$3.95.

A pink wool "Jones of New York" blazer—$4.50.

Once in a while I even spend more than $15.00 on an item. Here are some of those purchases.

A "Guy Laroche" red designer suit, fully lined and fully tailored—$19.99. For a dressy look, I added a cream-colored satin blouse inset with lace in a V shape. I purchased the blouse at an outlet in San Francisco for $35, rather than spending $75 or more in a department store.

A navy blue skimmer dress for summer—$24.95. The dress still had the manufacturer's tags in place. Two of the seven buttons were missing. Even if I had to replace all the buttons at $2.50 each, the dress was still a bargain. However, I was able to purchase, take apart, and basically manufacture a couple of buttons. I put them at the bottom of the dress and moved the two bottom buttons up to where the buttons were missing. No one knows the two at the bottom are ever so slightly different, unless I tell, and I'm not about to do that. I added to this outfit a pair of Lifestride sling pumps, navy blue with white toes and a blue and white striped button on the toe. I paid $4.95 for the shoes, and they were new, as proven by the unscuffed bottoms.

A new peach-colored linen suit—$26.00. The only thing wrong with this suit was that the lining of one sleeve was twisted. I opened up the seam and resewed it in about fifteen minutes. I added a black and white, polka dot shell and found a black and white polka dot oblong scarf (a previous thrifting purchase) in my accessory drawer. I gathered the scarf and fastened it with a rubber band to make a poof. This I pinned to a lapel of the suit. I added black shoes, black earrings, and a black handbag for a smashing look.

A couple of years ago, I needed a winter jacket. I spotted a red one that had wonderful lapels and pockets all over the place. I love red, and I love lots of detail such as unusual pockets and lapels. The jacket was new, and the price tag said $35. I knew this kind of jacket could sell for up to $200. I wanted it.

Imagine my dismay when I turned it over and found that because it was a salesman's sample, someone had intentionally cut a small square hole in the lower back to keep it from being sold at retail.

I left it hanging where I found it and walked out. But I couldn't forget it. Then I had an idea. Decorative patches are in style. What if I sewed a decorative patch over the hole? Would anyone ever know? It's a funny place for a decorative patch, but stranger things are done on commercial garments.

In a fabric store I found a decorative patch of black velvet with red designs that looked like a coat of arms. I bought two and then bought the jacket. I sewed one over the hole in the back and the other on the upper left jacket shoulder.

In the two years I have worn it, the only comment I have ever had was about the good looks of the garment. Once a man wanted to know what the patches stood for. (He had on a jacket covered with patches and was intrigued by mine.)

Once, while thrifting, I spotted a Gucci handbag sitting on top of a clothing rack. I couldn't believe my eyes. I thought it

101

must be an imitation, but there was the identifying trademark, and the leather straps, handles, and interior all bespoke quality. There was one problem, however. The zipper on the top was broken. Actually all that was wrong was that the teeth of the zipper had come out of the slide. The price of the bag was six dollars.

I quickly assessed the situation. Here was a one-hundred-dollar bag for only six dollars. Maybe the zipper could be replaced and maybe it couldn't, but if it couldn't, I wasn't wasting very much money. I decided to buy it.

I took it to a shoe shop, and they put the teeth back into the slide of the zipper for about three dollars. The only problem was, it didn't stay. They weren't very optimistic about replacing the whole zipper. They decided, instead, to put on a new slide. For another four dollars they completed the job, and I have been carrying that bag for several years now. Believe me when I tell you that you never know what you'll find in a thrift shop.

My thrifting adventures began many years ago, when we were so poor that families on welfare shared their surplus government food with us.

In order to clothe the children, I got boxes of scraps from my friends who sewed. From these I made dresses and play clothes. Often there was not enough of one kind of fabric to make an entire garment, so yokes and pockets of dresses were a contrasting color and sometimes edged or appliqued with the main fabric. The result was often more charming than if I'd had enough fabric for the entire garment.

Anyway, I discovered that thrift stores had not only fabric pieces big enough to make garments for the children, but for me, as well. They also had a large assortment of buttons, zippers, thread, and all the other sewing notions needed—for pennies. So I started buying these items.

One day, as I was on my way to the fabric area of the thrift store, I saw a little red coat with a black fur collar—size three. It was handmade, and had been exquisitely tailored. My mother had just given me a red velvet beret for my daughter, Wendy. The coat's price was $3.50. I bought it, and for over a year, she wore it and looked very smart.

Later on, when our son was due, I found a brand-new infant snowsuit for less than five dollars. It was then that I decided that if people were going to give and throw away wonderful items like these, I was going to find them and save money.

Because most children's clothing in this country is so well made and because children grow so quickly, there are lots and lots of clothes for them in thrift shops.

When buying children's clothing or anything else in a thrift store—or for that matter, anywhere—it's important to inspect it for damage. Stains and spots can be treated and often can be removed completely. Rit color remover is wonderful for removing stains on all white clothing and linens. Rips in seams, broken zippers, and missing buttons can all be fixed. Most tears in the fabric itself cannot be fixed inconspicuously, but maybe you can put an applique or trim over the tear. If you want a garment and it has stains you're not sure will come out, consider the price and ask yourself if you can afford to throw it away if you fail to remove the stain. Or could you live with it, if it were permanent?

Resale Shops

A close cousin to thrift stores are resale or consignment shops. I buy little in consignment shops, for two reasons. I almost never find the new items I find in thrift stores, and the prices of the used goods are higher.

Resale shops are places where patrons sell used items, usually clothing, for a 50 percent split with the shop owner. Good shops have strict rules about the kind of merchandise they accept—usually better quality, and it must be clean and pressed. There is often a time limit for selling the garment. If at the end of the allotted time no sale has been made, it is the patron's responsibility to claim it, or the shop owner will dispose of it.

Consignment and resale shops are big business where I live and probably in most areas of the country. Shops are listed in our local paper at least once a month in a group ad. Some of the shops' names are wonderful. There's Far Fetched, Your Hidden Closet, The Dark Horse Boutique, Ragamoffyns, and The Mouse Closet for infants and children.

Each consignment and thrift store takes on a personality of its own. I'm not sure why that is, but I know that I go to one thrift shop if I'm looking for handbags. They seem always to have an abundance of them. I go to another place if I want to do it myself and sew, for this shop has lots of fabric. Then there are the shops that have new clothes, good belts, and leather goods, and lots of silk scarves.

You learn which shops have more of which items by shopping them. I've found that if you go on a regular basis, you can determine what's new in a store in a few minutes and look at just those items. You don't have to look at everything every time. That would become overwhelming.

I also only look at clothing that is the right color for me. I never look at grays, beiges, or olive drab, because I know I can't wear those colors. I gravitate toward the true blues, reds, emerald greens, and pastels. That eliminates looking at tons of stuff.

In this chapter we're only talking about clothing, but later on we'll talk about resale and thrift shops as a source for furniture, small appliances, lamps, even vacuum cleaners.

Garage Sales

Garage sales are closely aligned with other thrift shopping. Garage sales, too, are the result of a burgeoning affluence in this country.

Garage sales can be great sources of children's clothing for the same reasons it can be found in thrift shops. Kids grow fast, and clothing is so well make it will last for several children.

A lot of the adult clothing offered for sale at these events is sadly out-of-date. This is the result of our tendency to hang on to the things we purchased that were mistakes in the first place. We somehow think that keeping them will make them become less of a mistake. It is also our tendency to think we'll lose ten pounds this year and fit back into that garment soon.

Maybe this is the best place to encourage you to look in your own closet for mistakes and outgrown clothing and have your own garage sale. Someone else could be using those items, and you could take the money you earn and reinvest it in better choices.

Swapping

Another way to acquire clothing for your family is to have a swap meet. A number of families get together and exchange items, particularly children's clothing. There might be a small price, or you might agree on no price for the items.

At the end of the swap meet, when everyone has chosen everything they need and want, call a local charity to come and pick up what is left over. Keep goods in circulation for maximum usage while they are in style.

Shopping in Your Closet

Sometimes all we need in order to have more clothes is a new way of looking at the old ones we have. Try taking everything you own out of the closet and piling it on a bed. Then pick up each garment and evaluate it. Ask yourself the following questions:

1. Does it fit?
2. Does it flatter me?
3. Do I like this color?
4. Have I worn it this year?
5. Is there any reason why I should keep it?

If the answer to all of these questions is no, discard the garment. Then take a look at the garments you have left. Try to determine why you like them, and remember for the next shopping trip. Try to look at your clothes in a new way.

Look at your suits. Could the jacket of one suit be worn with a different skirt or pants? Could the skirt or pants be worn with several other shirts or blouses? Would a new scarf or tie give you a whole new look? Could you mix dressy and casual clothes for versatility? Could you cut off the top of a dress and turn the bottom into a skirt to wear with other shirts, sweaters, and blouses? Could you top a dated dress with a jacket or a cropped top, add jewelry, belts, or other accessory items, and bring it to life? Could you mix prints or plaids to bring excitement? Could you mix color combinations you've never thought of before?

Sometimes buying one new item will give you dozens of new choices in your closet. For example, a good basic black, gray, or navy blue skirt or pants will mix with almost everything you own.

I keep wearing the same black skirt with a number of jackets, sweaters, blouses, vests, and so forth. If I want a new outfit, I usually only buy the top and use the same old skirt. A black skirt is a black skirt is a black skirt; there's not much you can do to change it. I have a couple, in fact, in different lengths and fabric weights.

Anything multicolored gives you lots of mix-and-match options. A trendy sweater with multicolors can be worn over almost everything you have. Recently, I bought a blouse with multicolored flowers all over it. I can't find anything I own that doesn't go with the blouse, except a plaid or another floral print.

Another device for shopping in your own wardrobe is organizing your closet so that you can find things. I use a system that is highly recommended by wardrobe planners: I group colors together. I hang all pants and skirts together in one place, but then they are hung by color families. I hang all blouses and all dresses in the same way. It's easy to find that certain blue blouse when you are organized this way.

Keep dressy clothes in a different place from the everyday wear. Put them at the back of the closet. Get some specialty hangers for belts and ties. There's no rule that says you can only have one belt hanger or one tie hanger. Get as many as you need to do the job for you. Be brave! Be creative!

Perhaps one, two, or even several of the ideas in this chapter will help you find more dollars for family fun. Clothing is one of the big-ticket items for families today. If we buy into the myth that it costs a lot of money to look great, we will spend our dollars on clothing rather than on experiences that will enhance our family life together.

Maybe what's in this chapter will spark creative ideas for you, as well. Don't stop with my ideas. Watch the supermarket magazines for money-saving tips on buying clothing. There are numerous articles every month on the subject.

What's on Sale This Month?

JANUARY

Appliances
Art supplies
Bedding
Blankets
Books
Carriages
China
Christmas gifts
Clothes dryers
Coats, men's
Costume jewelry
Dishes
Dresses
Electronic equipment
Furniture
Furs
Glassware
Handbags
Hats, men's
Home furnishings
Housewares
Infants' wear
Linens
Lingerie
Men's clothing
Men's shirts

Quilts
Rugs and carpets
Shoes
Sportswear
Stereo equipment
Storm windows
Suits, men's
Tablecloths
Toiletries
Towels
Toys
Water heaters

FEBRUARY

Air-conditioners
Art supplies
Bedding
Cars, used
Car seat covers
China
Christmas gifts
Clothes dryers
Curtains
Dishes
Drapes and curtains
Furniture
Glassware

Hats, women's
Home furnishings
Housewares
Lamps
Men's shirts
Radios, phonographs
Rugs and carpets
Silverware
Sportswear
Stereo equipment
Storm windows
Toys

MARCH

Clothes, spring
Clothes dryers
Coats, winter
Hosiery
Infants' wear
Laundry appliances
Luggage
Shoes, boys' and girls'
Ski equipment
Storm windows

APRIL

Clothes dryers
Coats, women's and children's
Dresses
Hats, women's
Housecoats
Infants' wear
Ranges
Suits, men's and boys'

MAY

Blankets
Christmas gifts
Handbags
Housecoats
Linens
Lingerie
Rugs and carpets
Television sets
Tires
Towels

JUNE

Building materials, lumber
Dresses
Frozen foods
Furniture
Housecoats
Piece goods
Summer clothes and fabrics
Television sets

JULY

Air-conditioners
Bathing suits
Children's clothing
Christmas gifts
Fuel oil
Hats, children's
Home appliances
Infants' wear
Lingerie
Men's shirts
Radios, phonographs
Refrigerators and freezers

Rugs and carpets
Shoes
Sportswear
Stereo equipment
Summer clothes and fabrics
Summer sports equipment
Toiletries
Toilet water and colognes

AUGUST

Air-conditioners
Bathing suits
Bedding
Carriages
Christmas gifts
Coats
Drapes and curtains
Fans
Furniture
Furs
Gardening equipment
Hardware
Home furnishings
Housewares
Lamps
Men's clothing
Paints
Rugs and carpets
School clothes
School supplies
Tires
Towels

SEPTEMBER

Batteries and mufflers
Bicycles

Cars, new
China
Christmas gifts
Dishes
Furniture
Gardening equipment
Glassware
Hardware
Housewares
Lamps
Paints
Piece goods
Rugs and carpets

OCTOBER

Bicycles
China
Fishing equipment
Glassware
Hosiery
Housecoats
School clothes
School supplies
Silverware

NOVEMBER

Bicycles
Cars, used
Car seat covers
Children's clothing
Christmas gifts
Coats, women's and children's
Dresses
Housecoats
Piece goods
Quilts

Ranges

Shirts, men's and boys'

Shoes, men's and women's

Water heaters

DECEMBER

Blankets

Cars, used

Children's clothing

Coats, women's and children's

Hats, children's

Party items

Quilts

Shoes

Family Adventures for Little or No Money

- Make fun hats out of paper plates and paper cups. Decorate them using felt-tip markers and stickers. Glue pom-poms, stars, buttons, or sequins on the hats.
- Spend time together looking at old family photos and telling the children what was happening when those photos were taken.
- Organize a neighborhood basketball tournament at someone's house, a school, or playground.
- Collect bugs and identify them by using a book from the library.

7

THE DECORATING SHOESTRING

A few years ago I met a group of women from Titusville, Florida, who really opened my eyes to the possibilities of decorating on a shoestring.

These women formed a team to help other women decorate their houses. Sometimes they helped a young woman who didn't have much money or much imagination; sometimes it was an older person who just couldn't do the painting and sewing anymore; and sometimes it was someone who just needed some new ideas. These women think of their efforts as a ministry. They charge nothing for their help.

Their plan of action is to come to a home and look it over carefully. They assess what they can use as it is; what can be moved to another room to work better; and what paint, wallpaper, and fabrics can do to make the house a more pleasing place to be. Then, on the appointed day, they come back in force—tools, paintbrushes, and sewing machines in hand—and in eight to twelve hours they transform the whole place. They sew, paint, wallpaper, clean carpets, move furniture, and make and hang draperies. They perform miracles.

These women use an abundance of fabric to accomplish their miracles, often sheets or sheeting fabric. In fact, Titusville has a sheet fabric outlet store. I'm sure these women are the store's best customers. They were making and hanging poofed valances long before they were popularly available ready-made. They design curtains with bishop's sleeves and crossovers and all kinds of other wonderful window treatments.

They don't believe any piece of furniture has to stay in the room for which it was purchased. If a corner cupboard works better in the bedroom than in the dining room, they may just move it there. These women gave me the courage to move a dresser, which had been purchased for use in the bedroom, into the dining room for use as storage for table linens. That particular house had lots of built-in storage in the bedroom, and there was no use for the chest there. It worked very well in the dining room. In the next house it was needed in the bedroom again.

All kinds of wonderful things can be done inexpensively if we can free up our thinking and begin to look at everything in a new way.

I have just purchased a set of old leather-bound encyclopedias, the fifth and limited edition *Encyclopedia Britanica,* published in Edinburgh, Scotland, in 1891. Besides being fascinating reading, these are beautiful old books. The leather is worn, some of the books have mildew damage, and on some the binding is coming loose, but they are still beautiful, and I have a plan for them.

Some time back, while shopping the furniture marts of Hickory, North Carolina, I saw a stack of books made from plaster of paris. The book stack was actually an end table. I thought, *That would be a great idea for a writer/editor's house.* But since that end table was very expensive, and since I didn't really like the colors, I didn't buy it. I did, however, tuck the idea away in my mind. I thought, *Why couldn't you do the same thing with real, old books?* You can pick up out-of-date leather-bound dictionaries, legal books, and other kinds of books very inexpensively. Why couldn't they be stacked up, perhaps drilled and a rod inserted to keep them in place? Then all you would have to

112

do would be to top them with glass and you would have a wonderful conversation-piece end table.

It's a great idea, except now that I have these books (I paid $20 for all of them), they are too old and too wonderful to drill, so I'm still thinking how I can make this project work. For the moment they are stacked up and topped with glass. It looks great, but it's a little precarious.

Free your mind to create new things from old things. Old pieces of oriental carpets can be made into throw pillows, colorful quilts can be hung on walls to cover plaster damage, old boots and shoes can be turned into planters for a patio, lace tablecloths can be hung for curtains, clever T-shirts can have the openings sewn shut and be turned into pillows for kids' beds, wonderful old teapots with missing lids can be stuffed with dried flowers to make beautiful arrangements. There is no end to what can be done. The clue is to begin to see things in a different way than you have in the past—to not limit your mind to what has always been.

Furnishings Set the Tone

We've gotten ahead of ourselves a bit. Let's go back and talk about basic home furnishings. The kind of home furnishings you choose is an expression of your family's life-style and interests. The way in which you furnish your house will tell visitors in a minute what kind of people live in this house.

I've gone into houses that were cluttered with books, musical instruments, pieces of half-finished artwork, and handicraft projects all over the place. It told me in a moment that the families who live in these houses may have a rather loose standard of housekeeping but it is certain that they enjoy creative endeavors.

I told in another book about visiting a home where American foxhounds were raised and sold. The walls were hung with ribbons, the bookcases were full of trophies, and on the table was an American foxhound, helping himself to the last of the family's dinner. That's not something I'd endorse, but dogs were

113

very important in this family. In fact, they were part of the family's livelihood.

I once had a friend, an older lady, who lived in a small mobile home near her daughter's house on a small farm. I'll never forget visiting her and finding a baby pig in a box in the corner. It was a runt and had nearly been abandoned by its mother. Belle had discovered its condition and brought it into the house. She warmed it in the oven and then wrapped it in blankets and put it in the box in the corner.

One never knew what one would find as part of the decor at Belle's house. Our children loved going there; it was always an adventure. Belle had learned the important lesson that things aren't as important as caring for God's creatures.

I've been in homes that were mini museums, where every item had been chosen because it was "right for the period." These homes and their furnishings reflected the interests of the owners and their investments of both money and time.

Homes where lots of chairs are drawn up around the fireplace in a tight conversational grouping and the TV is relegated to some other area of the house say that friendship, sharing, and conversation are important here.

Homes where the front hallway is crammed with skis, tennis rackets, bowling ball bags, and other sports equipment certainly shout loudly and clearly that here is a family to whom physical involvement in athletics is important. You'll probably find a large-screen TV tuned in to the sports channel. To get near it, you may have to thread your way across the family room floor, avoiding tennis shoes and hockey sticks.

A long time ago I read Edith Schaeffer's book *Hidden Art* for the first time. It had a profound effect upon my attitude toward all the aesthetic, sensory pursuits of life. It particularly had an effect on my attitude toward making a house a home. She emphasized the importance of making a home of anyplace you are sheltered, be it a castle or a hotel room.

She says,

It seems to me that, whether it is recognized or not, there is a terrific frustration which increases in intensity and harmfulness as time goes on, when people are always daydreaming of the kind of place in which they would like to live, yet never making the place where they do live into anything artistically satisfying to them. Always to dream of a cottage by a brook, while never doing anything original to the stuffy boarding-house room in a city; always to dream of a rock, glass and timber house on the cliffs above the sea, while never putting anything of yourself into the small village brick house; or to dream of what you could do with a hut in the jungle yet never to think of your inherited family mansion as anything but a place to mark time, is to waste creativity in this very basic area, and to hinder future creativity by not allowing it to grow and develop through use. Trying out all the ideas that come to you, within the limits of your present place, money, talents, materials and so forth, will not use up everything you want to save for the future, but will rather generate and develop more ideas.[1]

As soon as the front door of your home is opened, visitors will immediately know a lot about you, your family, and your lifestyle. How your home is furnished will indicate what is important in your life. Let me say here that there is no right or wrong way to furnish a home or to live. It is important that you find a style that is comfortable and right for your family and your situation. Children who are reared in a home where they are not allowed to sit on the furniture or touch anything are probably going to grow up to become either rigid and fussy about things or they are going to completely rebel and become sloppy and careless about possessions.

I had a friend who told me, when my two children were small, "Make just one room in the house off-limits to toys and general disarray. You need that to keep your sanity and to have a place to bring unexpected guests." I followed her advice. My living room was always open to my children, but they were encouraged to pursue quiet activities there, like listening to the stereo, reading, or drawing. They could not bring toys into the room and scatter them about.

The family room was just that—a family room where they could play with their toys to their hearts' content. At one time we had a "rec" room, which I often called the "wreck" room

115

because it looked like a wreck had happened there. I can't blame my children for all the confusion and mess in that room. I am an avid pursuer of craft projects, and sometimes the mess I made was bigger than theirs.

So what are the basic furnishings your family needs? First of all, remember that furniture is one of the biggest investments you will make in your lifetime. You will live with whatever you choose for a long time.

Few couples just starting out can afford to buy a whole houseful of furniture at one time, but they can put together a five- or ten-year plan and begin carefully buying a few pieces at a time. My experience has been that when one has to wait and save for a particular piece of furniture, there is more satisfaction and joy when you are finally able to buy it.

Think about pieces that you can buy now and use in one capacity or location that could later be used in another way or moved to another part of the house. Could you buy an area rug to use in your family room now and later move to a bedroom? I did that. I bought a large remnant rug and had it bound for the recreation room. Later, when we moved into another house, I had it cut down and rebound for the office. The scraps were bound as hall runners.

Now that I am thinking of building a third house, I'm thinking of having the largest piece dyed to fit my new color scheme until I can afford what I really want: an oriental rug. After that I'll probably put the piece in the basement area I hope to finish off someday.

If you are thinking about moving furniture or rugs from one area of the house to another, you need to coordinate color and style. Then the bright blue rug you've purchased for the family room will also work under the dining room table, in a child's room, or in a large hallway. A French Provincial cabinet can move from clothing storage in the bedroom to an extra storage chest in a hallway, to a teenager's bedroom.

When you are ready to make your first purchases, you should have thought your plan through thoroughly. You should have decided by that time what type and size furniture will look and work best for your family. Then purchase the most essential

116

pieces first. Probably the most essential piece of furniture is a bed. Start with a good mattress. (You spend a lot of the years of your life in bed.) You can put the mattress on the floor until you can afford a bed. Next buy a couch, table, chairs, a couple of good reading lamps, a dresser or chest of some kind, and a full-length mirror.

It is amazing what people will throw out or give away. You will probably be able to fill out your basic needs with purchases made at garage sales, thrift shops, secondhand stores, through classified ads, and even by watching what people throw away on community cleanup days. I once read about a man in New York City who managed to put together a complete set of original Hitchcock chairs just by watching what his neighbors put out on their trash piles. That happened a long time ago, and today people seldom throw away antique furniture, but they do still throw away a lot of good stuff.

Remember that well-made furniture frames can be reupholstered and solid furniture can be refinished or painted. Let me tell you about a couple of purchases I made that turned out to be winners. I bought a small upholstered armchair at the Salvation Army for fifteen dollars. Labels on the bottom of the chair indicated the chair had originally come from a manufacturer of high quality. The store label was still in place, and this told me that the chair had been purchased from a store that dealt in high-quality merchandise. The upholstery was soiled and an ugly color.

My son likes to tear apart old furniture, so he pulled the upholstery off the chair. I purchased about eight yards of fabric in a lovely print that coordinated with my existing color scheme and set about slowly reupholstering the chair. I put a layer of Dacron batting under the upholstery fabric to give the chair a soft touch. Then I found a beat-up old hassock and reupholstered it, as well. The end result was a lovely little armchair in just the exact colors I wanted, with a matching hassock. I had used a Laura Ashley chair as an inspiration. That chair sold for more than $700 with the hassock; my whole project cost $75.

Another time I found a Martha Washington armchair for six dollars. This time I got into a little more expense. Some of the rungs were missing, and I had new ones turned to match the existing rungs. Then I had the frame stripped and refinished professionally, since at that point in my life I had more money than time. Lastly, I had the chair reupholstered professionally. The total cost was $250, but that is a far cry from the ones I had seen in Colonial Williamsburg with a price tag of $700.

It is also possible to save money on quality furniture by purchasing unfinished furniture and furniture kits. These pieces have often been presanded. Some assembly may be required in addition to sanding and finishing. Stores and companies selling this furniture can give advice and sell you the products you will need to produce lovely furniture. If you are careful, you could end up with a piece of furniture that is better than commercially finished furniture. After all, yours will be hand-finished. It is important to work slowly and thoroughly and not ignore any of the suggested steps.

I have been amazed at the quality period reproduction pieces that are available from some catalog companies. One company advertises a cherry highboy in kit form for $3,400. The finished piece sells for $6,200. It could be that either price is too high for your family, or maybe you are not interested in this style of furniture. Just be aware that it is possible to purchase furniture in kit or unfinished furniture form and save a lot of money. In either case, what you end up with is a handmade piece, finished by you in just the color you desire.

What to Look for When Choosing Furniture

When purchasing furniture for a family, think comfort first—seating comfort and sleeping comfort. Then think about fabric. Can it be cleaned? How? Is this good basic design that can be reupholstered easily and therefore less expensively?

Early in my career as a homemaker, I met an interior decorator who helped me by encouraging me to buy the best sofa I could afford. It was a classic style. She further encouraged me to get it in a wonderful bright color rather than a drab brown or beige. She also helped me by giving me her decorator's discount.

I have enjoyed that sofa for twenty-four years. It has now been reupholstered for the third time. At the last change, I had the upholsterer change the style slightly to update it. It costs about $500 to have this sofa redone, a far cry from the $1,500 to $2,000 a new sofa would cost.

The two other times the sofa has been redone, I was able to pick up fabric at a bargain. For the first reupholstering job, I found a remnant fabric at a furniture factory in Indiana. This factory sold fabric by the pound. I think I paid $35 for the material. The other time I bought a mill end bolt of blue and white striped chintz for $15. After doing the sofa, I had enough left for a round floor-length table skirt, a bed ruffle, and two pillow shams.

Classically designed furniture makes good sense. Designs that have been popular for two hundred years will not go out of style next year. Once again, keep in mind that classic pieces can be used in many places and ways.

I have an antique hutch that has been used as a bookcase, a display cabinet for dishes, and a place to store office supplies. It could also be used in a bedroom to store sweaters and other clothing or in a hallway for linen storage.

If you lack ideas about how to make furniture do double duty, watch home-decorating magazines or take a tour of homes in your area. Interior decorators are not afraid to put furniture to multiple uses.

Where to Find Furniture

Perhaps you're thinking, *Where can I find furniture at a reasonable price?*

Your local furniture store will probably have a good sale once or twice this year, but did you know that these same furniture stores often have a warehouse where they sell one-of-a-kind pieces, last year's models, closeouts, and damaged pieces? I have not bought an appliance or a piece of furniture in a regular store for years. Not only are prices cheaper at the warehouses than in the stores on an everyday basis, but the warehouses get overstocked sometimes and have sales. When that happens, prices are often cut from 50 to 70 percent.

I've found a source where I can *truly* save money on quality furniture: the furniture markets and outlets in eastern manufacturing towns. In particular, I have discovered the furniture manufacturing area of North Carolina.

It has been my privilege to travel there a number of times in the last ten years. North Carolina is my ancestral home, and I began going there about five years ago to visit my great aunt, then in her nineties. At that time I started shopping the furniture shops around Hickory. There I discovered amazing bargains. When I know I am going east, I try to save my money so that I am ready to buy.

The dealers in such towns as High Point, Thomasville, and Lenoir, North Carolina, are most accommodating. They have a system for efficiently delivering the furniture you order to your doorstep. The shipping charges are fairly reasonable. Even after you add the freight, your savings are still considerable.

If you cannot go to North Carolina to buy furniture, there is another way to reap the benefits of these wonderful discounts. All you have to do is to go to your local furniture store and pick out what you like. Get the model numbers, fabric name, and so forth. Then look in the back of almost any decorating or home magazine and find an ad that says, "Buy furniture direct from the manufacturer." Often there is a toll-free number to call. Call and tell them what you want. They'll figure out a way to get it for you. They'll give you an exact price for the piece and tell you exactly what the shipping charges will be. There will be no surprises.

The last time I bought furniture this way, I was required to get two cashier's checks, one for the furniture itself and the other for the freight. I had them waiting when the furniture was delivered.

Another wonderful way to get top-quality furniture at bargain prices is to watch for furniture stores going out of business. Many times I have purchased top-of-the-line furniture for the dealer's cost. The last time this happened, it was almost unbelievable. There wasn't much left on the display floor, but there was a large stepback pine hutch painted a colonial red color. There were also four Windsor chairs in the same color and two side chairs in a colonial blue-green color.

I didn't realize what we were looking at when I first came into the store. I knew I needed some good chairs and these looked sturdy and well made. In fact, they were handmade, as was the hutch. The hutch had originally retailed for $5,000. Each of the Windsor chairs retailed for $625, and the two side chairs retailed for $750 each. We made a deal with the store owners, who were anxious to get rid of everything and close the door forever. For $1,000 we bought the entire lot. Eight thousand dollars worth of furniture for $1,000. Amazing!

How Can I Know Excellent Quality?

As in most things in life, the best way to learn what true quality is, is to keep looking at it. Have you ever heard of someone who found an old masterpiece in an attic or hanging on some wall, forgotten by all who pass by? How did that person recognize the treasure? By being able to recognize quality through looking at quality.

This kind of training is easy and inexpensive. It comes by visiting museums and art galleries and taking the tours that are offered. It comes by touring old houses and antique galleries and talking with the proprietors of those places. It comes by reading and mostly by just paying attention—being fully alive to life.

When you have trained yourself, you may someday find yourself at a yard sale or a thrift shop or at the demise of some estate and suddenly discover that once-in-a-lifetime treasure. It happens to people like you!

Here are some guidelines for recognizing quality in furniture:

1. Check the joints of drawers. They should be clean and tight fitting. Quality furniture will have dovetailed joinings.

121

2. Drawers should slide smoothly.

3. Furniture doors should be well hung and fitted.

4. Backs and undersides of furniture should be of wood and should be finished.

5. Check the finish. It should be smooth and of an even application.

6. Check the hardware. Is it appropriate to the piece? Is it the same quality as the piece? Is it firmly attached?

7. For upholstered furniture, ask to see literature or a model that shows how the interior of the piece is made. Stuffing can cover a massive amount of poor workmanship.

8. Buy well-known brand names from reputable stores. If the prices seem too high, save and wait for the really big sales.

9. Most upholstered furniture does not have a warranty. The exception is mattresses, which are usually guaranteed by the manufacturer for ten to twenty years.

What about Floor Coverings?

There are lots of options in floor coverings. Once again, it is important to consider the lifestyle of your family. If you have a house full of sports enthusiasts who are tracking equipment, grass, mud, snow, or other unmentionables into the house on a regular basis, you might want to consider using a lot of easy-care, no-wax vinyl flooring.

I have a friend who loves animals and always has five to ten living with her. She says, "I just have to have one room in my house that has easy-care, wipe-up flooring, so that I can care for a sick animal."

If you love beautiful old furniture, it will show up best in a room with solid wood floors and area rugs. Wood floors come in softwood and hardwood. Pine flooring is quite soft, and while it is very beautiful, it will dent from high-heeled shoes or dropped items. It also wears down more quickly and must be refinished more often.

Hardwood floors, on the other hand, are usually white or red oak. They, too, will dent, but not as easily as softwood floors. I love hardwood floors because they are very beautiful and I find them very easy to care for. I prefer something called a Swedish finish, which requires (infrequently) a quick wipe with white vinegar and water. In between times, a quick swish around the room with a dustmop keeps them lovely.

Of course, the all-time favorite for floor covering is wall-to-wall carpet. It's a favorite for a number of reasons. One is the warmth underfoot. Another is that carpeting reduces noise (wooden floors can be very noisy). Since the advent of man-made fibers for carpeting, wall-to-wall rugs are quite easy to care for, and they come in a wide range of colors, styles, and patterns—something for every income and taste.

In choosing carpet, buy the best you can afford. Here is a place where it really makes sense, in the long run, to buy quality. Quality carpets have a longer life and do not need to be replaced as often; they are made of better fibers and will not take as much care; the colors will not fade with repeated cleanings or exposure to sunlight; they will not pill up, mat, or otherwise become unattractive.

One mark of a quality carpet is its density. The way to check the density of a carpet is to fold a piece of it in half, back to back. If the fibers on the surface are still thick and it is hard to see the backing, you are holding a good piece of carpet. But if, on the other hand, there is a space between tufts of fibers and the backing is all too easy to see, you are holding a poor-quality piece. Price, unfortunately, is another way to check for quality. High-quality carpeting costs more than poor-quality carpeting.

Carpeting should be installed over the best grade of padding you can afford. Padding gives a cushioned feeling underfoot, and more important, padding extends the life of the carpet.

Carpet should be purchased from a reputable dealer and should be installed by a reputable installer. This is not the place to make any major mistakes. There is too much money involved.

There is a new idea in carpet sales, called mobile service. The dealer will come to your home not only with carpet samples, but with a video camera. He takes a picture of your room

123

and then, through the magic of computer technology, he shows you how various kinds and colors of carpeting will look on your floors. You don't have to go to a local carpet store and be overwhelmed by choices. You don't have to wonder what that color carpet will look like on your floor. You don't even have to leave the comforts of your home to see, decide, and set up all the arrangements for the installation of carpet in your home.

What about Appliances?

I have a hard time getting excited about appliances, but that's probably not a good attitude, since they can eat up a huge hunk of a furnishing budget. We need to know what we are doing when we buy appliances.

Appliances are our friends, our helpers—the workhorses of our existence. Once again, it is important to determine what your family needs in terms of appliances. I wrote about that in my book *Finding Time for Family Fun.* Let me quote here:

We all need some basic tools to use in our home—things like a good can opener, great knives, a vacuum cleaner, basic garden tools. We need appliances to help us with our work. We need to buy the best appliances we can afford, but we probably don't need to buy top-of-the-line appliances to get the job done. A simpler, less complicated appliance may work better and in the long run avoid costly repairs.

Buy only the convenience you need in an appliance. Every added convenience is one more thing that can break down. Ask yourself:

1. What do I really need in an appliance?
2. What extra items would save me time and what ones are nice but not needed?
3. What will it cost me when I buy the machine to add those items?
4. What will it cost me at the time of repair to have those extra items?
5. Is this machine easy to clean and care for? Give some careful and serious thought to the kinds of appliances you will pur-

124

chase. Do your homework. Check consumer reports to see which is the best for the money spent. Often it is not the most expensive appliance.[2]

Here are some guidelines for buying appliances:

1. Don't buy on impulse. Plan your purchases.
2. Don't buy more than you need. Buy no-frills.
3. Buy when the appliances are on sale.
4. Shop for model closeouts, markdowns, and so forth.
5. Find out if the appliance will fit where you want to put it.
6. Consider whether it will be large enough for future needs as your family grows.
7. Find out what the purchase price includes. Does it include delivery? set-up? warranty? service? And if so, for how long?
8. Find out the average life expectancy of this appliance.

It is possible to save money on appliances by buying second-hand. Watch the newspaper classified ads for these items. Most appliances are very heavy and add significantly to the cost of moving to another part of the country. People often opt to sell their appliances rather than move them, even though these items may not be too old and they may take a considerable loss.

Remember that the expected life of a washing machine is eleven years, so a washer that is only five years old could have at least six years left, and probably more. A clothes dryer is estimated to have at least a fourteen-year lifespan, although in my experience it is the dryer that wears out first.

When buying used appliances, you will be buying "as is," and there is a risk involved, but even extensive repairs will probably cost much less than the price of new machines.

Buying used goes for appliances other than washers and dryers. People often replace stoves and dishwashers when they remodel and are eager to get rid of the old ones. Freezers and refrigerators are as difficult to move to a new location as washers and dryers. Used ones are advertised in the classified ads almost every day of the week.

I bought a secondhand freezer for fifty dollars. I used it for a number of years, and then it began to leak air around the door seal. I thought it was the end of the road for the freezer but then I heard how to fix it.

I pulled the seal forward and filled it with caulking material. This forced the door seal toward the freezer itself. The test was to close the freezer door on a dollar bill wedged between the door and the freezer. If the seal was tight enough, it would be difficult to pull the dollar bill out of the closed door.

I tried this all around the seal. Where it was easy to pull it out, I added more caulking. That old freezer lasted another eighteen years. One day I discovered it had died and I said, "That was one great old freezer. They don't make them like they used to. I'm going to let it rest in peace."

I guess we had the freezer about twenty-five years altogether. That means the purchase price, spread over the period of time we owned it, was about two dollars a year. It is possible to find good value in used appliances.

Accessories

Accessory items—lamps, pictures, pillows, and so forth—are the jewels of your home. They are the little touches that give your home your style and make it unique to your family's personality.

Accessory items can be very expensive. You can literally spend a fortune on them, but it isn't necessary to do so. We are living in a time when handicrafts have made a resurgence, and it is easy to buy them in shops, at fairs, and at craft shows. It is also possible to learn how to make them yourself.

My friend and I were at her parents' home. I was fascinated by the hooked rugs my friend's mother was making. She had been making rugs for a number of years and had refined the craft to an art. Talk about recycling. This lady buys old wool skirts for her craft. After she washes the wool, she dyes it the exact shade she needs. Then she cuts the fabric into tiny strips with a cutting tool, and then hooks the fabric into a backing to make wonderful handcrafted rugs.

It is possible to buy a loom and learn how to weave all kinds of wonderfully patterned fabrics. It is possible to learn to make lace and woodworking projects. Recently a popular magazine had instructions for making a small, rustic table out of twigs cut from trees in your own yard.

Most people collect something. I've been picking up black and white china dogs for my son for years. I collect red and white pottery. My daughter collects hats and other costume materials.

Most children collect rocks, shells, birds' nests, and other natural items. These items can be viewed as junk or messy collections or they can be displayed in some attractive way and kept as "treasures of childhood." I have jars of various kinds of stones, shells, crystals, and beach glass we picked up over the years. I bought some inexpensive storage jars with pretty tops. The collected items look very pretty in them and make a nice accessory for a bathroom or in a window where the sun shines through the crystals and beach glass.

A collection of birds' nests would look very pretty in an open hutch. Along with a couple of simple birdhouses, they would make a very nice country display.

Your choice of accessory items will only be limited by your imagination. Each person in a family should have some input as to the decoration of a home, and each person should have some space that is just his. Children, as soon as they are old enough, should help decide on the decor and accessories of their rooms. They may not do their rooms the way you would, but it is important that they have a place to express their own taste.

For small children, put shelves low enough so they can put their accessory items (which will be stuffed animals and other toys) where they can see them. They are not going to observe much that is above their eye level. Low shelves will also encourage them to put away their toys by themselves.

The possibilities for making a shell of a house a true home are unlimited. Just pick up any home-type magazine in a super-

127

market today and your mind will be boggled by the possibilities. Create a style that is unique to your family and your way of life. Choose a style that lets your family relax and be at home. Make it a place where all your friends and their friends love to come and share a meal.

I've been encouraging my now grown-up children to make their apartments a home, because "If you don't make a home, you will never be home." They are beginning to do that. We all need an island of peace and quiet where we can retreat from the hubbub of life and be safe.

The next few pages will give you lots of good, quick, money-saving ideas for home decorating.

Ideas for Saving Money on Home Decorating

Furniture

1. Watch the classified ads for items you need. These may be sold through garage sales or directly to you. Always offer less than the asking price; you might be amazed at how little you will pay.

2. Look in your telephone directory's Yellow Pages for resale and consignment shops that sell furniture and accessory items.

3. Search out warehouses that sell one-of-a-kind or close-out models. Get on their mailing lists for twice-a-year sales. Watch newspapers and television for notification of these sales.

4. Visit auctions. Most auctions have an inspection time ahead of the actual event. Take advantage of that time and inspect the items carefully. If you don't know how to buy at auction, go with someone who does and observe and learn before you begin bidding.

5. High-quality furniture stores have excellent sales several times a year. Learn when the item you want will be on sale.

6. Buy from furniture marts in East Coast manufacturing towns, either in person or by phone. This can be facili-

tated by ordering the *Wholesale-by-Mail Catalog 1991* (Lowell Miller and Prudence McCullough [New York: Harper and Row, 1990]).

7. Shop unfinished-furniture stores for high-quality furniture at a reasonable price. Sometimes you can buy finished model pieces for less than in a regular furniture store.

8. If you cannot afford the latest in upholstered furniture, get good used furniture and slipcover it in the upholstery of your choice. Upholsterers can make slipcovers for you. They are very stylish, but can be almost as expensive as reupholstering the piece. Or you can make the slipcovers yourself. Vogue patterns, as well as other pattern companies, have very simple patterns for slipcovers.

9. If the upholstery is in good condition and you can live with the color, add lots of accessory items—pillows, matching table skirts, valances, and so forth. Chances are your family and visitors won't even see the upholstery.

10. Make a full-length cloth for a round table. You can put anything with a round top under such a table skirt. It is possible to purchase pressboard rounds with legs that screw on at fabric stores and through mail order catalogs. Mine is a round of plywood screwed to an old nightstand. I've used it for many years as a bedside table in the bedroom and as a lamp table in the living room.

11. Paint furniture if the finish can no longer be restored. Stencil designs on the painted furniture for a fresh country look.

12. Watch for ideas for building simple furniture for the family room and other casual areas of your home. It is fairly simple to build a banquette by building a low box with a platform top and then adding a single mattress, bolsters, oversized pillows for the top. Add an upholstery slipcover to the mattress.

129

13. Investigate a simple slipcover treatment for outdoor wire chairs, folding wooden chairs, and so forth. By adding a simple slipcover, you can transform these utilitarian items into lovely indoor decorator items. Some of the slipcovers have big bows in the back, which make them charming for a bedroom or a little girl's room.

Accessories

14. Make country throw pillows from plaid dish towels or bandanna kerchiefs.
15. Glue four six-inch tiles together at the corners with tacky glue to make a lovely cachepot.

Paint and Paper

16. Paint stools in bright colors for the kitchen. Paint on cow patterns for a fun look.
17. Experiment with sponge-painting techniques. You can attain some interesting results on furniture, walls, and ceilings.
18. Paint terra-cotta pots in matching colors. They will not be as porous and will hold moisture better. Prime them before painting.
19. Paint galvanized buckets for the kids' rooms. Add decals or paint on fun pictures, which could be taken from their coloring books.
20. Cover an old foot locker or trunk with gift wrap or maps. Add a dozen coats of shellac for a rock-hard finish that will last for years.
21. Watch magazines for patterns, stencils, and ideas for painting furniture and adding decorative borders to walls.
22. Investigate the lovely finishes that can be achieved through color washes.
23. If you can't afford a carpet or rug for your bare floor, paint a design on it. That's what early settlers did. Use

a checkerboard pattern or stencil a design directly on the floor.

24. Use decoupage to disguise damaged furniture finishes.

25. Paint a checkerboard cloth design on an outdoor picnic table for fun.

Outdoor Furniture

26. Old wheel rims from cars can be welded together to form stools for the patio. Weld two wheels together, spray paint, and add a cushion top. Or use two wheels welded together and add an outdoor plywood top for a low patio table. More rims welded together would add more height and could be used as a regular patio dining table. These have plenty of weight and will not blow over in the wind.

Miscellaneous

27. Check out the pattern books in fabric stores for patterns for valances, curtains, pillows, and a multitude of other decorator items.

28. Think about ways to use your doors and walls for storage space. The backs of doors can be used to store magazines simply by adding a rack.

29. Use sheets and pillow ticking for decorative fabrics. Use lots of these fabrics for a luxurious look.

30. Use a section of picket fence in the opening of a fireplace. Bank it with potted plants or real or artificial greenery for a fresh summer look.

31. Cover damaged walls with fabric. Some use a light padding behind the fabric for a luxurious look. Seams can be covered by gluing braid over them or by adding simple wooden trim painted a matching color.

32. Pad and upholster a headboard of a bed to coordinate with the bedspread and other fabrics used in the room.

131

Decorating for Christmas

33. Use cookie cutters as ornaments for the tree, or hang them on a cord strung across a window. Cookie cutters come in bright colors, copper, or silver.

34. A big wooden bowl of cookie cutters with a few shiny balls tossed in makes a nice decoration for a kitchen or family room.

35. Have your children make paper snowflakes. Tape them to a window and spray artificial snow through them to transfer the pattern to the window.

36. Glue interesting pasta shapes together to form ornaments. These can be spray painted gold.

37. Heap a wooden garden tool carrier with pinecones. Tie a bright plaid bow to the handle. Put it in a hallway.

38. Use the same wooden tool carrier without the pinecones as a place to put Christmas cards. Keep it in the living room or the family room. Encourage your children to enjoy the cards.

39. Spray paint pinecones in white and gold and pile in a gilt basket for a table decoration.

40. Spray paint bay leaves a golden color and add them to a bowl of potpourri for a festive look.

41. Thread shiny balls and pinecones onto a velvet ribbon and use it to tie back drapes.

42. Hang a tiny birdhouse on the side of the house or the wall of a room. Add some greenery and a plaid bow.

43. Stalks of wheat tied with a bright red velvet bow makes a nice decoration for the outside of a house and a great gift for the birds.

44. If your children like to collect birds' nests, bring them out now. Some can be set on the branches of the Christmas tree. Others grouped together will make a lovely buffet display when mixed with greens, red berries, and tiny bows. Fill the nest with wooden eggs.

45. Use cut greens as bouquets. Put them in interesting bottles, pots, brass or copper buckets, or just about anything you have that will hold water. Cut evergreens kept in water will last throughout the holidays. The greens can be sprayed lightly with glue and brushed with glitter that looks like frost crystals. Add a red velvet bow for a look of elegance.

46. Wreaths and swags can be made from almost any imaginable substance. Of course evergreen and holly wreaths are traditional and very nice, if you can cut the greens yourself. But you can also wire brightly wrapped Christmas candy to a styrofoam ring. Use old-fashioned hairpins to do this. Attach a tiny pair of children's scissors to the wreath with a ribbon for cutting loose the pieces of candy.

47. Use pasta in bow tie and wheel shapes to make a kitchen wreath. Glue the pasta as close together as possible on the styrofoam base.

48. If you live where you can buy them reasonably, use hot peppers wired together to form a Southwestern wreath.

49. If you live where you can get it, wire bay leaves together to form a delightful-smelling wreath.

50. Poke loops of ribbons that have been wired at the bottom into a styrofoam base as close together as possible to completely hide the base. You can also attach the loops of ribbons with pins.

51. Make a wreath using loops of cornhusks. You may need to soften them in water to bend them into loops. Mix the cornhusk loops with calico ribbon loops.

52. Form a wreath of baby's breath and greens. Encircle it with lots of tiny lights.

53. Use collectibles such as seashells for a wreath. Glue them to a styrofoam base or add to greens.

54. At the end of the Christmas season, watch for Christmas china. It doesn't have to be expensive, and after the hol-

133

idays, it should be available for half-price. It will make your holiday table special.

55. A centerpiece can be a bowl of red and green apples. Tuck in stick cinnamon tied with tiny red plaid bows.

56. Use the children's teddy bears for a corner display. Tie Christmas bows around their necks. It doesn't matter if the bears are worn.

57. Let the children string cranberries and wind them with greens to make a garland for doors, windows, or a lamppost.

58. Use a child's sled for a fireside or doorside decoration. Add some greens and a bow or two. Even an old snow shovel can be turned into an outdoor Christmas decoration by adding a big plaid bow and a bunch of greens. Put it right by the front door.

59. Make simple Christmas stockings from elegant tapestry remnants—or use velvet, lamé, or other luxurious fabrics. Add lots of metallic trim, sequins, or embroidery done with gold thread.

60. Remember that food is beautiful. Display Christmas goodies in clear glass jars and other storage containers.

Family Adventures for Little or No Money

- Plant grapefruit, lemon, orange, or apple seeds. If they are not a hybrid variety they will sprout. Suspend an avocado seed in water by inserting toothpicks in the sides to hold it in place. Do the same with various kinds of potatoes.
- Check out videos from your library for an evening of video fun.

8

WHEELS

A couple of years ago, between buying Christmas gifts for my kids and buying milk, I decided to stop off at a local car dealership, just to see what they had. I had my heart set on a red Honda Prelude. Of course, I hoped I could get it with a full accessory package.

I began my conversation with the salesman by asking him about the Prelude on the showroom floor. I quickly ascertained that I was not going to be able to afford the car. But as all good car salesmen do, he assured me that such cars keep their value and began to describe a used Prelude that had come in earlier that day.

As I listened, I began to realize there was something he was not telling me. I said, "What color is that Prelude?"

"Red," he answered.

"Is there some reason you're not showing it to me?" I asked.

"Well, it's on the back lot. Some people were looking at it."

"Did they put money down on it?" I asked.

"No."

"Can I see it?"

He took me out, and I slid behind the wheel of my dream car. It was four years old and had 25,000 miles on it, but I didn't care, because it was $9,000 cheaper than the new one on the floor and had everything I wanted—air-conditioning, sunroof, four-wheel steering, quadraphonic sound with equalizer. In fact, I couldn't think of one more thing I would want to add.

"I suppose you want to drive it," he said.

"Yes, I sure do!" I told him.

I drove it, loved it, and then said to the salesman, "Is there any reason I can't buy it?"

"No," he said.

And so I bought it on the spot. Well, I made the down payment. I'm still paying off the rest. The car is everything I had ever hoped for, and I hope it will last forever. Up until then, I had driven the family "junk car." I was thrilled to have my own dream car.

I'm not unusual. We Americans continue our love affair with the automobile, despite the fact that they cost more than we could ever have imagined a few years back, despite the fact that gasoline and repair costs keep escalating, and despite the fact that insurance costs are out of sight.

An automobile is the second most expensive item in the family budget, the first being a house. Because a car seems to be the extension of many people's personality, and because the purchase of a car is a highly emotional experience, we tend to forget some of our financial skills, throw caution to the wind, and buy what we love. Then, later on, we suffer the consequences of our actions. Sometimes we find we've spent too much for the car or we haven't bought a car that meets our family's needs. By the time we realize our mistake, the car has already begun to depreciate. To avoid these kinds of problems, we have to think and plan ahead.

It's wise to save for a car and pay cash. By paying cash you will realize a major savings on interest payments. I didn't follow my own advice, and I realize now that one or two month's car payments are for interest. That's a lot of money to give away.

Ron Blue says, in his book *A Woman's Guide to Financial Peace of Mind*, "If you can't afford to save for a car, you can't

136

afford to borrow for it, either. If you believe this, it means you will drive the car you now own a little longer, or wait a little longer to purchase a first car."[1]

Do You Need a Car?

Of course, you need a car! Is there any question about it? Yes, the question should be asked. The best way to save money on car expenses is to not own a car. Most of us truly do need a car, but there are some of us who could do without one. In fact, there are many people who have figured out a way to do without a car, and they manage quite well without car payments, insurance payments, gas fill-ups, and all the rest.

If you live in a city with a good transit system, it may well be that you can use it to get everywhere you need to go. In fact, in some cities a car is a real liability. If you live in an apartment or condominium, you need a place to park your car. Sometimes apartment complexes have parking; sometimes they don't. Often the only parking spot is outdoors or perhaps even on the street, where the car is subject to all kinds of damage.

If you live in a city and drive to work, you have to navigate the traffic, deal with the fact that you are contributing to pollution, and find a place to park at work. In some cities, places to park are almost nonexistent or so expensive that you might feel you are making a daily investment in urban real estate.

If you choose to commute by public transit, what do you do about those times when you truly need a car? Splurge and call a cab or a limo. It's cheaper than paying car-related expenses. Rent a car for a trip or vacation. What could be nicer than taking a family trip in a brand-new car? Weekly rates for rental cars are fairly low, compared to the cost of owning a car.

But even when all the logic is understood, most of us will still want to own a car for the flexibility, independence, and mobility it gives our family. In that case, maybe we should think about the possibility of owning less car. Think about buying a good, small used car and paying cash for it. Perhaps it would be all you need for errands and short family trips. Maybe commuting could be done by public transportation and your family could rent a full-size car for that once-a-year vacation.

Think it through, and don't buy more car than you need to provide adequate transportation for your family.

How Many Cars Do You Need?

This is a question that is born directly out of our affluence. In most countries of the world, there is no question about owning even one car, but here we wonder how many cars we should have.

The answer to the question is easy: Don't own more cars than you need. Once we lived in the suburbs of a city that had no public transportation, and we had only one car. I usually had to walk where I wanted to go, or wait until evening to use the family car. Fortunately, we weren't too far from a grocery store, so it was possible to walk there and bring home a few groceries.

But it wasn't easy to be without a car. Once I walked two miles to a bus stop. That took about forty minutes. Then I waited another forty minutes in the cold for the bus, which was running late. I boarded the bus only to find that it stopped at almost every street corner. What would have been a twenty-minute car trip turned into a half-day event; and the worst part was that when I got as close to my destination as I could, I was still a couple of miles away and someone had to come get me. I was not too happy.

So there definitely are times when the possession of a second car makes life easier. But what should that second car be? Take a look at your life-style. Do you need a station wagon to transport the ball team? Do you need a small pickup to haul yard debris or furniture? Do you need a small car for running errands? Is your family filled with sports enthusiasts who need to tow or top-carry boats, skis, bicycles, or other gear? Or are you, like me, thinking about the need for a four-wheel rig to get through the snow?

Think about the interests and activities of your family and buy only what you need. That need may change as time goes on. You may have wanted to pull a trailer at one point in your

138

life and later on decide to stay in hotels. You may have lived where you needed a snow-friendly conveyance, and now you've moved to the desert. Life changes; needs change. So if you see that you now own more car than you need, sell it and buy less.

Buying the First Family Car

I like buying new cars. I like shopping for different models, doing the research to determine which car uses the least gasoline per mile, investigating which cars need the least repairs and how expensive those repairs will be when they are needed. I like determining how big an engine is needed and what accessory items are essential and which would only be wonderful to have. I want to know what the resale value is on a particular model.

Whenever possible, buy a new car for the number-one family car. Dependability is important in a family automobile, so if you are going to have a car for your family, buy the best you can afford.

Someone in the family needs to do research on different kinds of cars. Research can be done through reading automotive magazines and consumer reports, talking with dealers of various kinds of cars, and talking with people who are satisfied with the car model you have chosen.

One of the reasons I wanted the car I bought was that I had done all the research and found it met all of the criteria. I also had a friend who had an identical car and loved it. I am so satisfied with the car I hope it never wears out; but if it does, I hope I can buy another just like it. Now that's satisfaction!

How Long Should You Keep the Car?

Many people buy a new car every two or three years. They feel it helps them keep up with the depreciation factor. But others like to keep their cars longer, pay them off, and have a small respite from car payments. Remember that if you are saving for a new car, you are also accumulating interest on the money you are putting in the bank. Ron Blue says, "If you take out a loan to buy a car like most people—you'll be on the wrong side of the magic of compounding. Instead of earning interest on your savings, the bank will be earning interest on your payments. Lenders know this, which is why they're so ready to loan you money."[2]

Ron also says, "Research shows that absolutely the cheapest car you will ever drive is the car you presently own. The cost of replacement and the incidental costs of a new car far outweigh the repair and maintenance costs of an older car. It's never advantageous from a purely economic standpoint to replace your car."[3]

Sylvia Porter agrees. She says:

> The year-by-year per-mile averages in the tables also emphasize the fact that you, as an annual trader, pay more for your car than you do if you keep your vehicle longer. Owners of ten-year-old cars pay only about three-fifths what the annual trader is spending. . . . Despite the folklore about old cars costing more than new ones, this simply is not so. . . . It is never cheaper to trade in a car rather than repair it and keep it!
>
> Maintenance expenses do rise in later years—often quite sharply in the sixth through tenth years of the vehicle's life. But these increases in upkeep costs are more than offset by the lower depreciation charges in later years.[4]

Studies have shown what it costs to buy a new car every one or two years as opposed to keeping a car for a decade. Look for this information in the popular money books that are available.

If you decide to drive your car longer, then regular servicing of the vehicle becomes even more important. Perhaps nothing extends the life of a car more than regular oil and filter changes. It may seem like an unnecessary expense, and you may be tempted to forget it, but this is an expense that avoids many problems with your automobile. Other servicing, such as regular lubrication, emission adjustments, and air filter changes, also help extend the life of a car.

If resale is important to you (and it should be), then it is important to take care of the finish and interior of the car. No one likes to buy a dirty used car, unless it is very cheap.

We once bought a very dirty used car for only $900. It was a full-size sedan with automatic everything and air-conditioning. It had new tires and an extra set of snow tires on rims. We were about to take a coast-to-coast car trip, and our regular family car did not have air-conditioning.

The people who had owned this car were heavy smokers, and the interior of the car showed it. There were yellow nicotine stains everywhere. My dad, bless his heart, got in and scrubbed and scrubbed and eliminated most of the stains. We even had to take the dashboard off and get rid of a layer of ashes behind it.

The car was the right price, and it met a particular need at that time, but we never did completely get rid of the smoke smell in that car. Because we lived where it was possible to have the windows of the car open or the air-conditioner turned on most of the time, we got by.

That car turned out to be a great buy. Not only did we take a 6,000-mile trip in great comfort, but various members of the family drove it for the next eight years. It finally died as a victim of inflation—it was a real gas hog.

The point is, if you want a high resale value on your car, take care of it both inside and outside. The closer to new it looks when you sell it, the more you will get for it.

What Kind of Interior Is Best?

When buying a new car for a family, it is important to think about the upholstery. Although none of us would complain about real leather or plush seats, try to think what they will look like after Suzy mashes a cookie into the upholstery. Children are messy, in case you hadn't noticed. They spill things, chew things, track all kind of unmentionables into a car, and can even get sick in a car. Perhaps for a family, good old vinyl seats are the best investment.

How to Shop for a Car

The way to shop for a car is probably not the way I did it— dropping into a dealership between the Christmas gifts and the milk and buying a car. A better way is to visit several show-rooms, talk to the salesmen (who will be only too happy to talk with you), look at the various models, test drive several kinds of cars, do your research, and then make your decision.

The whole business of test driving a car is very important. Take the car for as long as the dealer will allow. A car may seem comfortable to drive and ride in for the first half-hour, but after that, it may become increasingly uncomfortable. A compact economy car is not a good buy if you are miserable the whole time you are riding in it.

Everyone in the family who will be driving the car should come along. Let them evaluate the maneuverability, handling, ride, visibility, ventilation, and whether the gauges and controls are easy to use. Take the car on the freeway to check for interior noise. See if the car has enough acceleration power to pass slower vehicles easily. How does the car handle on curves and in traffic? When a passenger is comfortably seated in the front seat, is there room for someone to sit in the backseat? What happens when the little people in your family grow to be big people? Will there still be room for their legs? Will there be headroom for them and everyone else? What will it be like to load and unload cargo from this car? Will there even be room for cargo, or will you have to attach a top carrier, which will seriously increase gas consumption?

Ron Blue tells how he taught his daughter Cynthia to buy a car. First he had her visit several dealerships to determine what features she wanted in a car. Then Ron and Cynthia went back to the dealerships together, to determine what the initial offer from the dealers would be. Then they began bargaining. They asked salesman number one for the best price he could give them, then went to salesman number two and asked him. They visited several dealerships and got their best price. Then they went back to all of the previous salesmen and told them the best price they had been offered. In every case, the salesmen lowered their price, until eventually no one would lower the price any farther. Cynthia finally paid about 15 percent below the sticker price.[5]

Getting the Money to Buy a Car

This is not as big a problem as it should be. Car loans are relatively easy to get. Dealers don't seem to care if you put a huge down payment on the car or if you finance every dollar, but you should care, for the reasons we've already discussed.

Put the biggest down payment you can afford on the car and try to repay the loan in the shortest time you can. This will probably make your monthly payment quite large, but you will save substantially in interest.

Some dealerships have package deals for loans, whereby you finance the car through their own finance company and get your insurance at the same place. Package deals are usually not such great deals. Shop separately for financing and insurance.

Talk to your own banker—the one you've established credit with over the years. Your own bank wants to keep you as a customer and will therefore do their best for you. Their advice about your loan will also be given from the standpoint of a long-term relationship with you, their customer.

Alternate Forms of Transportation

Transportation comes through various kinds of conveyances, and we need to talk about transportation in something other than cars. In recent years many people have begun to ride two-wheeled vehicles to work.

Motorcycles, bicycles, and mopeds can all be used as transportation. I shall never forget being in downtown Manhattan, waiting for a stoplight to change so that a group of us could cross the street. A small motorized scooter of some kind, something like a moped, cruised up to the light and stopped. I looked around to see an elegantly clad young woman braking for the stoplight. When the bike stopped, she put a foot, encased in a very beautiful high-heeled suede pump, down to steady the bike. She seemed quite unconcerned with the huge trucks and tangle of cars surging all about her.

Many cities have been and are constructing bike lanes to accommodate bicycle traffic in a safe manner. Biking is an economical means of transportation, and after a few miles of commuting by bicycle, one does not have to be concerned about additional aerobic exercise.

Think about it. Nonmotorized biking does not pollute the atmosphere, provides aerobic exercise, is inexpensive, does not contribute to traffic congestion, and it can sometimes be quicker than a car in traffic.

As with everything, there is an up side and a down side to this solution. What does one wear to bike to work? If there is a place to change at the office, you can wear regular biking clothes. Of course, that means taking a change of clothes with you, and that can be a problem, too.

Where do you put your bike when you get to work? Some people remove the front wheel and chain it and the entire bike to a post. Some offices allow bikes in a storage area or in an out-of-the-way hallway. This is probably something that more companies concerned about the environment need to think about.

If you can find a way to commute to work by bicycle, it can be a great saving of money. If you can't, perhaps you can encourage your children to ride their bikes more.

Studies that show how little exercise our children are getting these days are frightening. Children need to be encouraged to be outdoors, playing, exercising, and even working. One of the ways they can do this is by riding their bikes to and from activities.

It is also frightening to learn how many young people are crippled for life by head injuries. Bicycle, moped, and motorcycle riders must wear helmets. When you buy your child his first bike, also buy a helmet and insist the child wear it at all times. That helmet may be the most important piece of equipment you ever buy your child.

Another wise investment is a bicycle safety course. Often these are provided by schools, local police or traffic officers, and by city park and recreation departments. Children must know the rules of the road in order to be safe. They must know where they can ride and those roads that are unsafe.

Since biking is such great exercise and recreation for the entire family, think about investing in bikes for everyone, then teach your child about safe biking by going with him and setting a good example.

Speaking about bicycles and thinking about saving money, let's talk about where we can find bicycles at a good price.

First of all, the same rules apply here as they do to a car: Don't buy more bike than you need. Holland probably has more bikers, per capita, than any other country in the world. When you go to an outdoor market or to a shopping mall, the outside of the area is jammed with bikes. None of them are chained up, and almost all of them look alike. They are plain, black, without gears, and everyone—from old grandmothers in babushkas to little kids—rides these bikes. Of course, Holland is a very flat country.

The point is, in Holland a bicycle is a valuable means of transportation, but the Dutch don't make a lot of fuss about owning fancy bikes. They also don't seem to worry much about anyone stealing them.

Here in the United States, secondhand bikes can be purchased at garage sales, through newspaper ads, or in thrift and secondhand shops. Bikes are something children eventually outgrow, and everyone has to dispose of them. Since bikes are basic, old bikes can be revived by the purchase of new tires, a good servicing at a bike shop, some scrubbing, and perhaps some paint.

Watch for local police auctions. Police pick up abandoned and stolen bikes on a regular basis. Once or twice a year, they will hold an auction and sell off these unclaimed bikes. You can purchase a really great bike for a minuscule price.

Mopeds and motorcycles are in an entirely different league than bicycles. I have known people who think motorcycle travel is the most exciting travel in the world. I have met couples in campgrounds traveling double on a motorcycle and pulling a little trailer with all their camping gear. They go thousands of miles and love the feel of the wind in their faces, the economy of this means of travel, and the complete freedom they feel when traveling by bike.

These are not roughnecks or hoods—they are ordinary businessmen and women, homemakers and executives, parents and kids. Although I am not an aficionado of the motorcycle, it bears looking into for some families.

We seem destined to have wheels under us, and since we are, it is wise to give serious thought to cost, safety, convenience, and wise environmental consumerism.

Family Adventures for Little or No Money

- Go sledding or tubing with the family.
- Have a family walkathon. Each person should select a walking-distance goal according to his or her age. Post these on a chart by week or month. Have family members record their daily walking distances.
- Let the older kids go on a scavenger hunt. When they return with their treasures, have a special treat waiting for them—their favorite pizza or sundaes.

9

TRAVELING WHEN YOU CAN'T AFFORD IT

One of the happiest times of my childhood was probably one of the most traumatic for my parents. Dad's company arranged his work schedule so that he made shift changes every two weeks. He worked the day shift for two weeks, the afternoon shift for two weeks, and the night shift for two weeks. When he was on the day shift, he would get up at 4:00 A.M. and be home by about 3:00 P.M. When he worked the afternoon shift, he went in about 12:30 and came home long after I was in bed. When he worked the night shift, he left about 9:30 P.M. and came in about the time I was getting up in the morning.

That was the bad part. He must have had something akin to jet lag most of the time. The good part was that every once in a while this rotating schedule would give him four or five days off in a row. When that happened, all five of us would go to some nearby place for a minivacation. Usually it was a camping trip in the north end of our county near the Bob Marshall Wilderness area of Montana. I remember what a happy, wonderful summer we had together.

We never had very much money when I was growing up. Mom was a full-time homemaker until I was in junior high school. At that time she took a part-time job. Yet we traveled more than most families—all of it by pickup truck. Dad built a camper on the back of a pickup truck long before anyone was manufacturing campers or pickup shells. We kids would ride in the camper, stretched out on a bed. What fun times we had, laughing, talking, fighting, and when the road was rough, bouncing up and down on that bed!

Anyway, we did a lot of camping and visiting friends and relatives for our family vacations. We never stayed in a hotel, and we never felt underpriviledged because we didn't. We didn't know there was any other way to do things, and we got to go more places than most of our friends.

When my children were small, we followed basically the same system. We never had a lot of money for travel, but we loved to travel, so we found ways to economize without giving us all a feeling of unreasonable penny-pinching. That's what this chapter is all about: how to get out and travel economically with your family, without feeling deprived. My ideas are only a starting place. Magazines, books, travel guides, and free brochures will give you dozens of other options, and don't forget the very best source of inexpensive travel information—your friends, especially those with children.

Where to Go

Where to go is probably best determined by how much money you have available for traveling expenses. It takes lots of money to fly a family to a foreign destination. We did that once, and it was a wonderful experience, but we had some other fun vacations that cost only a fraction of what that one did.

It takes a considerable sum of money to put a family up in a luxury hotel at a theme park, unless you can find a great travel package. It takes a lot of money to spend several weeks on the road, traveling across the United States. But then, I doubt if I need to tell you that. If you have children, you've probably already looked into all of the expensive ideas for travel. What you want to know are the alternatives.

First of all, don't overplan for the age of your children. Little children most enjoy your attention and your company. They don't care where the interaction takes place. It can happen in your backyard. The problem with backyard vacations is that parents usually see all that needs to be done and never stop working, so interaction with the children doesn't take place.

If your children are small and you want to go somewhere, pick a place with lots of sunshine and some water, preferably near home. Maybe you can rent a cottage at a lake or ocean-side. Many of these cottages are fully equipped, so all you have to bring are your clothes and play equipment. Most have kitchens, and since families have to eat even if they stay at home, it doesn't cost any more to eat here than it would at home.

If a family is economizing by doing its own cooking, it is important that all able-bodied people get involved in the cooking and cleanup. *Mom needs a vacation, too!* Perhaps to ease the strain of cooking, some meals can be eaten out, depending on your budget.

This simple kind of arrangement works well for small children, for several reasons. Children get very tired and cranky on long car trips. Sometimes their parents do, too. Why do that to yourself or the child? Drive somewhere less than two hours away from where you live. Set up a homelike atmosphere and schedule. Put the children to bed at about the same time. (The first night might be tough because of their being in a new place.) Get up at about the same time. Eat the same food that you eat at home, to avoid crankiness and upset stomachs.

The big difference should be that you and the child can go out to the stream and throw rocks or splash about in the water. You can search for rocks and shells and interesting bugs, or an unusual leaf or stick. You can read stories while sitting in the sunshine, or if it rains you can stay inside and watch the rain through the window, sit by a fire, or play games together.

Together is the key word here. Whether Dad and the boys are washing dishes after a meal or Mom and the girls are riding

149

mopeds down the beach, the key is being and doing things *together.*

I recently read an article that talked about the difference in American and European vacations. Americans tend, the article said, to keep on the move while vacationing. I remember seeing a funny cartoon where a family had stopped at Yellowstone Falls in Yellowstone Park. One person in the family was snapping a picture, and a child sitting in a car was asking, "What is it?" The answer was, "I don't know, but I've taken a picture. We'll look at it and figure it out when we get home."

That's too true to be funny. It's all too typical of American vacations. Run! Run! Run!

On the other hand, the article stated that Europeans tend to go to one location and stay there for three or four weeks. I can verify this. When we pulled into our first campground in Dijon, France, on a vacation we took in Europe, it was amazing to see the marvelous camping apparatus the Europeans had.

There were big tent cottages spread out on the grass. There were travel trailers of every imaginable kind. Sometimes European families spend the entire summer in such a place. The worker in the family goes home during the week and returns on weekends to spend time with the family.

I noticed that the European campers pulled up their lawn chairs in front of the tent or "caravan" and talked, sang, and laughed far into the night. We could probably learn something important from our European neighbors about how to recreate and rest.

There are some families who have an "always" place. Sometimes it's a family cottage where they go to escape the rigors of life and be with members of the extended family. Sometimes it's a certain vacation destination—a certain cottage, a certain suite in a certain hotel, a certain campground. There is stability to that kind of vacationing that might be right for your family.

One word of caution. Because so many of us choose to live far away from our parents and families, we often think vacation time means a visit to the grandparents' house. It's important for your children to know their grandparents and be able to benefit from the influence of their lives and experience. It's important that children get a sense of their history from their grandparents. But what often happens when parents and grandparents get together is that children are left out of the conversations. They would have been better off at home. It is important to take time for your children—one-on-one—when you are visiting relatives. It's important to arrange your schedule so the child has one-on-one time with each of the grandparents. I'm very aware of this because I've been so guilty of talking over the heads of my children, almost ignoring them when chattering away with my folks or other family members.

When your children are older, extend your vacation plans. If they are old enough to walk, you can plan day hiking, city walking, backpacking trips, or other walking activities. There is no better way to see what's there than to get out and walk. Have you ever driven up and down the same street for months and seen little, then one day take a walk along the same street and be amazed at all that is there?

I'll never forget being in Yellowstone Park and overhearing a tourist say, "There's not much here, is there?" Not much here! There's so much in Yellowstone Park that you could spend a lifetime studying it and never understand it all. The secret is getting out of the car and taking walks on the safe, paved walkways. The park officials can't move all the geysers, bubbling paint pots, roaring fissures, and steaming pools to the side of the road, although every endeavor has been made to bring the highways as close to them as possible.

When your kids are old enough to walk—and before they think the only way of moving is with wheels under them—get out and walk, and see a little of the world.

Save the touristy kind of stuff for when the children are older. I don't know what happens to kids as they grow older, but they finally reach a point when they want to do all the uneducational, natureless, mechanical stuff they can find.

I remember being at Niagara Falls. What awesome beauty! What unbelievable power! What a tourist trap! After properly viewing the falls, Wendy, then in her late teens, said, "I want to do the tourist trap junk. I want to go to the wax museum, the believe-it-or-not-place, and all the other stuff." And so she did.

151

Set Goals for Family Travel

You can probably go any place you make up your mind to go. You can probably vacation any place you want to, if you save for the trip, make it a top priority, plan ahead, decide to do it economically, and have patience to wait for the right time.

You'll never know what you can do together as a family until you make some goals. There's nothing wrong with children contributing some of their earnings to make a family vacation happen. There's nothing wrong with having a garage sale and getting rid of the excess to make it happen. There's nothing wrong with someone getting a part-time job or setting up a cottage industry to make a special family vacation a possibility. In fact, those times when everyone has worked together to make a special trip come about may be more memorable than when Dad shells out all the money for the trip.

Start building a file of places your family would like to go. Each year, usually in the spring, the popular supermarket magazines have articles about family travel. Clip those and file them for future reference, or purchase a travel magazine and look at the little ads in the back. You'll find ordering information for brochures and maps—more information than you can ever use. Most of it is free. If they're old enough, let the kids send for the information. They'll learn how to do research, have fun getting the mail, and be involved in the planning process, which will make the vacation very special to them.

In tight economic years—and we seem to be having a batch of them—it may be hard to justify including a family vacation in your budget. But it may be more important then than ever for your family to get away from the day-to-day stress of trying to make ends meet. Your family may be desperately in need of time for rebuilding emotional ties to one another.

Where Will You Sleep?

Decide to take a vacation, even if funds are tight. Decide, too, how much you will spend for a place to sleep. There are many options for inexpensive accommodations.

Find a beautiful spot and rent a two-bedroom cottage with kitchen facilities (usually forty to seventy-five dollars per night). The savings are significant because you can sleep up to six people and save even more by cooking your own meals.

Go to popular tourist areas in the off season and save big bucks. The summer months are off-season in Florida; Disneyworld is in Florida.

Summer is also off-season for well-known ski areas. Check out Snowbird, Utah, Sun Valley, Idaho, and other popular ski areas all over the country.

Swap your home with another family through a home-exchange program. Some people find this an exciting way to see a new area of the country without the cost of hotels. There are exchanges available in Hawaii and even internationally. Contact Vacation Exchange Club (VEC), 1-800-638-3841, for more information.

National parks offer inexpensive places to stay. Many of our national parks have wonderful old hotels and lodges that are relatively inexpensive. Because they are old, sometimes the accommodations are also dated. I remember that at Old Faithful Lodge in Yellowstone Park, it was necessary to go down the hall to the bathroom. But the place had charm and was inexpensive, which made up for the inconvenience. The lodge also had rooms with full accommodations at higher prices.

Think about tent cabins. Some national parks (Yosemite, for one) have a trail-hiking system that includes tent cabins and tent restaurants set up at intervals along the trail. You can hike five to ten miles and have a place to stay and eat without carrying any equipment. The full length of the trail is about fifty miles.

National parks also have woodsy cabins, tepees, luxurious hotels, and campgrounds—something for every taste.

State parks also offer inexpensive lodging. The Oregon state park system is one of the finest in the country. Each ocean campsite offers something in addition to the ocean, beach, and campsites. Usually there is a naturalist who presents a nightly program. There are visitors' centers and interpretive displays set up in many of the state parks.

153

Most state parks also have water and electrical hookups for campers, hot showers, and other amenities to make you forget you're camping.

Since national and state parks are so popular, make reservations several months in advance of your intended vacation time.

A recreational vehicle may be the answer for your family. I remember sitting in a tent campsite in a state park and seeing the longest recreational vehicle imaginable being squeezed between pine trees and finally maneuvered into a campsite. I thought to myself, *There is living, moving proof that you can take it with you. You can take all of it with you.*

Friends who have camped in recreational vehicles for years tell me it's the only way to go. That may be true. A recreational vehicle will give you great mobility and variety in where you can stay. As I've mentioned, you can stay in state and national parks, but there are also campgrounds in almost every city and village in the country. Most of those are right in or near the city, near a park or a body of water.

Recreational vehicles are another way to give children a sense of stability while traveling. They sleep in the same bed every night, hang their clothes on the same hooks every day, and eat their meals at the same table, even though the vehicle may be parked in a different spot every day. This kind of routine avoids a lot of upset and confusion in their lives.

If you don't think you would use a recreational vehicle enough to warrant owning one, you can rent one. The rental rate for a week ranges from $400 for a simple model to $1,200 for the luxury version. Remember that recreational vehicles consume a huge amount of gasoline, so figure that cost into your vacation budget, as well.

Let's Go Camping

Many American families with young children have discovered the joys and agonies of camping vacations. One thing for sure: Once your equipment is purchased, camping is probably one of the least expensive of all vacations. If you refrain from taking along more than you actually need, you can probably get by with hauling the equipment in a top carrier or even in the trunk of your car.

If I have expertise in any kind of inexpensive family vacationing, it is in the area of camping. I've done it most of my life. Sometimes I've loved it. (Who could do anything else when you step out of a tent on a crisp early morning to find a deer browsing in the meadow nearby and the sun just beginning to touch a snowcapped mountain?) Sometimes I've hated it. (Who wouldn't hate it when hail pounds the top of the tent and it begins to leak and you go out in the night to investigate what's happening and step into six inches of ice-cold water and mud?)

We have two adult children. One of them still loves camping and frequently plans camping trips for her friends. The other hates camping and only stays in nice hotels.

I do believe, however, that camping is great training in problem solving. It introduces so many problems that the whole process makes children grow into young adults who are able to cope in almost every travel situation.

I'm the world's laziest tent camper. I also love my comfort. Tent camping, comfort, and laziness can all go together.

Over the years of rearing the family, we had two different kinds of tents for two different purposes. One tent was a nine-by-twelve cabin tent, the size of many rooms. We bought the tent used and paid thirty-five dollars for it. (Lots of people give tent camping a try and then give it up. You can buy their equipment cheap.)

After we picked a campsite, set up the tent, rolled out our two-inch-thick foam pads and fluffy Dacron sleeping bags, we were at home. It didn't matter if the tent site was beside the ocean, a mountain stream, a sagebrush flat, or in Switzerland: once we closed the flap on the tent, we were home.

I always made it a policy to eat the same kind of food we ate at home. Picnic food is all right for one meal, but on an extended vacation, it can cause all kinds of problems. Instead of a constant diet of potato salad, baked beans, hot dogs, potato chips, and pickles, we ate what we normally ate at the dinner table at home. Early in our camping experience we invested in a good propane stove and a good-size tank for the propane. The stove

155

folded up to the size of a briefcase, and a tank of propane would last through a vacation.

I got so I could set up the stove and have a meal ready to eat in twenty to thirty minutes. I've cooked not only in campgrounds, but in roadside rest areas, city parks, and almost every other place I could find a flat surface to set up the stove.

I usually tried to buy fresh meat late in the afternoon for the evening meal. (This is also a good time to replenish the ice supply in the cooler box.) We would eat the meat either by itself, if it was steak or meat patties, or incorporate it into a one-dish skillet meal. The meal was filled out with salad or fresh fruit, cooked vegetables, and a simple dessert. I always had a backup meat ready—such as canned chicken—in case we couldn't get to a store.

Breakfasts were made up of some combination of cold cereal, pancakes, omelettes, or scrambled eggs. While I made breakfast, I also made lunch and packed it in a back pack. Anything that might spoil was kept in an ice chest and taken out when needed. By fixing lunch at the same time I fixed breakfast, I was through with food until the evening meal—and that only took about thirty minutes.

To further aid my laziness, I used paper plates tucked into rattan plate holders. I prefer real silverware to plastic, so we used stainless steel knives, forks, and spoons. This also made cleanup easy, because as soon as a meal was cooked, I put two enamel pans of water on the camp stove and then used the top of the stove to wash the dishes. It was easy to plunk the silver, glasses, and cups right into the hot water, give them a quick wash and rinse, and spread them out on a towel to air-dry. Some campers put everything in a net bag and hang it on a tree or tent pole to dry.

I stored silverware in one of those tubes potato chips come in. It was just the right size. I also found it was easier to find the implement you were looking for if forks and knives were stored point down and spoons were stored bowl up. Other implements for cooking were very few (see the list at the end of this chapter).

You can save on food for camping trips by planning ahead and watching for sales on prepackaged items. Any kind of packaged pasta or noodle dish can be mixed with a number of different meats for a quick meal. Buy canned whole chicken for a chicken and dumpling dinner or for chicken and noodles. Buy small hams in cans and other canned meats.

For one summer's camping I bought, on sale, individual hot-chocolate-mix packets, premeasured packages of orange breakfast drink, one-serving packets of mashed potatoes, a hot syrup mix, dry milk in one-quart packets, and iced tea mix in premeasured packets.

To save storage space, remove all the ingredients from each box and repackage them in plastic bags. Be sure to include the cooking instructions from the box.

I like to prepackage all the ingredients of a meal into one bag. For example: Put a noodle dinner in a small plastic bag, then put that bag in a larger one, along with a can of boned chicken, tuna, or salmon. Put in a can of vegetables or freeze-dried vegetables, available from almost any outdoor supply store. You might even include drink mixes and tea bags. Label the bag with the day you intend to use it. You don't even have to think about what to eat on a particular night of a camping trip. What could be easier?

Let your kids get involved with meal planning and prepackaging of food. It will be great training for them. They can help cook it at the campsite, too, if they're old enough.

Since a vacation is supposed to be a time to free your mind, I like to plan my menus ahead of time, on cards. When it's time to pack the food, it is easy to make sure everything is in. It's very freeing to know dinner is planned and all the ingredients are together.

Whether you are camping or economizing by cooking some of your meals on a long driving trip, remember that there may be long days when you will be too tired to cook or bad weather that forces you indoors.

I must tell you a story about cooking outdoors in bad weather. We were traveling in eastern Montana. The sky had been threatening rain for hours, but we thought we could outrun the storm.

157

We stopped at a roadside rest area that had roofed picnic shelters. Dinner that night was steak, green salad, potatoes, and a dessert.

All went well. Dinner was very enjoyable, except for the approaching clouds we were all watching. The storm hit just as I started washing up. Hailstones as big as golf balls bounced off the roof of the shelter. Rain poured in through its slatted sides. We put up the plastic tablecloth to try to keep some of it out, but it didn't do much good.

After about ten or fifteen minutes, when we were thoroughly wet and growing very cold, the rain began to abate just a little, and we sent the kids running for the car. They had to wade through eight inches of water to reach the car.

No camping out tonight! We were a sodden group as we checked into a motel later that evening. When we flipped on the news, we heard there had been a tornado exactly where we had been eating dinner. The announcer advised viewers not to go outdoors. We didn't know whether to laugh or cry.

Allow flexibility in your budget, your time, and your attitude for overtired kids and spouses, bad weather, and "I just want to do something different."

I am a strong advocate of stopping along the road for a meal, which can be as simple as a sandwich. The kids can run off some of the steam that has been building while sitting still in the car. Bring a frisbee, a ball and bat, badminton rackets (forget the net), or some other small game items. Let them run and play. Parents need to run and play and exercise, too.

One more word about food and little people: They get hungry, they get bored, and they need snacks. Plan their snacks. Aseptically packaged drinks or drinks in squeeze bottles, raisins, whole-wheat crackers, prepopped popcorn, and "gorp" in small packages are great treats.

Gorp is any combination of nuts, seeds, raisins, chocolate bits and pieces, and dried fruit that your family likes. While it is high in calories, it is also high in nutrition.

Or perhaps, instead of serving desserts with a meal, save them for roadside stops. Look for a fresh-fruit stand or a frozen

158

yogurt shop. Try to avoid candy, ice cream, soda pop, and high-calorie, high-fat chips.

Packing for a Trip

Always strive to take less. When you have a small child, that is almost impossible. Whether it's a bassinet or a portable crib, a baby buggy or a stroller, a potty chair or a half-ton of diapers—or all of the above—you get the feeling you are carrying an entire nursery in your car. Don't forget the bulky car seat, etc.

During this period, I learned how little I could get by with. Each trip, I took less and less for myself, until now I can take a three-week overseas trip with one small backpack and a camera bag. I could travel for three months with the same amount of equipment, although I might have to buy something along the way to keep me from going mad from wearing the same three sets of clothes.

Here are some general tips for cutting down on the amount of stuff you take on a trip. Observe what flight attendants carry and how. Wear your heaviest clothes—a suit or other two-piece outfit. Make sure the pieces of the suit coordinate with everything else you are taking. The jacket should coordinate with other slacks or skirts. The skirt or pants should mix with sweaters, shirts, or blouses. Carry a lightweight raincoat; one with a zip-out lining is best. The raincoat can double as a bathrobe, if need be.

In selecting a wardrobe for a trip, I always base everything on one color. If the basic is a black skirt or slacks, then all tops and jackets coordinate with that black skirt. One of my favorite color combinations, because I never tire of it, is red, white, and blue. It always seems fresh to me. I want my wardrobe so well coordinated that I can reach for any top and any bottom in the suitcase (in the dark) and know they go together.

Take two other skirts, slacks, or jeans in dark colors, to cut down on washing. Take two or three lightweight (easy to dry) tops, then add a lightweight wool sweater.

Be sure you have a good pair of walking shoes that are well broken in and comfortable. Take one pair of dress shoes and a pair of sandals that can triple as beach shoes, slippers, and casual street shoes.

Take about three or four changes of underwear, socks, and panty hose for each person in the family. Add some kind of sleepwear for each person. When our two children were teenagers, they were most comfortable sleeping in a T-shirt and shorts. Be sure to take a clothesline and pins, so you can wash out your clothing.

More can be put in less space if you roll clothing, especially cotton knits, undergarments, and sleepwear. Fold clothing items smoothly and then roll them up.

Keep cosmetics and toiletry items to a minimum. Decide on just one set of makeup and use it with all costumes. Repack all toiletries in unbreakable, lightweight plastic bottles.

Take along some basic first-aid supplies. I usually take along adhesive bandages, antiseptic ointment, antidiarrheal medication, laxatives, aspirin, vitamins, motion sickness medication (if appropriate), and any daily medications. Beyond that, you can stop at a drugstore or see a doctor.

Money-Saving Ideas for Travel

There are thousands of ideas for money-saving travel. Here is a potpourri of them:

1. Stop at state welcoming centers and pick up brochures that tell you where the best bargains are to be found in recreational ideas, places to stay, and even bargain shopping.

2. When making reservations, always ask for the best discounts.

3. Investigate traveling by train and bus. Amtrak and United Airlines have a package deal that allows you to take the train one way and fly the other. A train trip could be a great adventure for your kids.

4. Look into Amtrak's All-Aboard America plan, which gives you unlimited travel with three stops over a forty-five-day period.

5. Eat out in the best restaurants, but do it for breakfast or lunch. These meals are less expensive.

6. Limit your eating out in restaurants and plan it into your budget.

7. Some theme parks have reduced ("twilight") fares later in the day.

8. In a large city you can sometimes rent a furnished apartment for a week. This is considerably less expensive than paying big-city hotel rates.

9. Investigate bed and breakfast inns. There are books that list B&Bs all across the country. Make sure kids are welcome. Remember, breakfast comes with the price of the room.

10. Investigate hotel chains that let kids stay in their parents' room free. Book early.

11. Go to the zoo. Most are either free or very inexpensive. Even if the zoo charges an admission fee, it may have a free day.

12. Visit art galleries and other museums. They are either inexpensive or free.

13. Visit factories that have free tours. Make arrangements ahead of time.

14. Visit state capitol buildings. They are often filled with history, and there is usually a guided tour.

15. Visit historic cities such as Williamsburg, Jamestown, or Yorktown, Virginia. Get out and walk through these wonderful old restored areas.

16. For other city walk ideas, check out Frommer's City Guide books.

17. Contact Family Vacation Services, Inc., 1-800-762-3872, for a complete listing of free vacation brochures by categories: dude ranches, theme parks, water activities, resorts, adventure.

Camping Equipment

Tent

- Poles, stakes
- Tent
- Axe or hammer for pounding stakes
- Ground cloth for under tent

Sleeping Gear

- Sleeping bags
- Foam pads, rolled up, or air mattresses
- Small pillows in dark-colored cases
- Air pump, if using air mattresses
- Flashlight

Cooking Gear

- Stove
- Propane tank
- Ten-inch frying pan
- Three nesting cooking pots
- Locking pliers
- Pancake turner
- Large spoon
- Vinyl tablecloth
- Tongs
- Pot holders
- Enamel dishpans
- Ice chest
- Serrated knife
- Stove lighter

- Detergent
- Scouring pad
- Water container
- Thermos
- Can opener

Food Staples

- Salt and pepper
- Small amount of flour
- Small amount of sugar
- Shortening
- Oil
- Menu items

Eating

- Paper plates
- Rattan plate holders
- Paper napkins or towels
- Thermal cups
- Nesting glasses
- Silverware
- Small plastic bowls with lids

Clothing

- Rain gear
- Stocking caps
- Coats
- Wool sweaters
- Swimsuits
- Shoes
- Personal clothing

Fire Making

- Kindling
- Fire starters
- Matches

Dry Goods

- Small rug for the front of tent
- Dish towels
- Dishcloths
- Towels
- Facecloths
- Soap
- Mirror

- First-aid items
- Toilet paper with core removed to conserve space

Bikes

- Bikes
- Bike rack
- Lock and chain

Fun and Games

- Frisbee
- Kite
- Games (small ones)
- Books

Family Adventures for Little or No Money

- Put up a tent in the yard and have everyone sleep out. You could pretend you're on a safari or that you're pioneers moving west. Read stories together in the dark by flashlight or lantern.
- Take the family to free workshops that museums sponsor.
- Go on a rock hunt. Pick up interesting rocks and classify them with the help of a good rock book from the library.
- Things to do at a stream: skip rocks on the placid parts; turn over rocks and see what's under them; sit quietly and watch for birds such as kingfishers, water dippers, and herons. Teach your children to be observant.
- Walk through an empty lot and look for useful discarded items. Think of ways to use your finds. (Don't limit an item to its original use.)

- Put together an old-fashioned radio drama with all the family participating. Record it and then play it back on family night.
- Save funny articles, cartoons, and photos. Laughter is good medicine for families.
- Read to your children the books listed in the back of Gladys Hunt's book *Honey for a Child's Heart*. Reading together as a family will build memories you'll treasure forever.

10

GET IT FREE

Yesterday I went to a concert given by one of the best bands in the country, the United States Air Force band. They played a little patriotic music, a little movie theme music, a little Dixieland jazz, and a little big-band music. It was wonderful, and the price was right—it was free.

I know most of you don't live where you can enjoy the air force band for free, but you do live where some musical events are free.

Free Musical Events

I grew up in Deer Lodge, Montana, population 4,500. Deer Lodge is the home of the state penitentiary. Not much of a claim to fame, is it? For all of my growing-up years, I remember hearing the prison band playing on Sunday afternoons, but it was a long time before I knew the band gave concerts on Sunday afternoons. I'll never forget the first time I went to a concert there. I looked up to see a slogan painted on the plaster just above the stage. It read, "Do not abandon hope." I also remember the clanging gates as we were locked into the prison with the prisoners.

The point is, Deer Lodge, Montana, is a little tiny mountain town, and you can still find a free concert there—if you don't mind being shut up with prisoners.

Most big cities hold free concerts in parks during the summer. Seattle's symphony holds what are called "brown bag concerts" downtown in a park known as Freeway Park, which is, as you might expect, built right over the freeway.

Other sources of free music are local colleges. Music students are required to give performances for their degree. They would love to have an audience come to hear them perform. Their music, while quite structured, is well rehearsed. It has to be, if they are going to graduate.

There are all kinds of other free musical events. Some restaurants feature a musician. I can think of a favorite restaurant where a truly superb pianist plays every Saturday morning. The place is packed. And I can think of another restaurant where a guitarist plays classical guitar.

Free Theater

Free theater might be a bit more difficult to find than free music, but in many cities around the country there are theater-in-the-park programs that are free. Not free, but very inexpensive, are the dramatic presentations of high schools, colleges, and local theater groups.

I always think of civic theater as groups of neighbors getting together to put on a play for other neighbors. It reminds me of when I was little and we dressed up to have a performance for the neighborhood kids or our parents. It may not be the best acting in the world, but it is fun.

Of course, the ultimate free fun with the theater is to get involved in it yourself. I know a family with four children, now almost grown, who have from time to time all been involved in productions, sometimes individually and sometimes as a family. Think of the fun it must be for the whole family to be in a play together.

If not all the members of your family are actors, then there is always stage production, costuming, stage managing, and being in charge of the lighting.

Swapping

Swapping (not swap meets) has almost become a lost art. Maybe it's because we tend to live in splendid isolation. Maybe it's because we all have so much money we can just toss out the things our money has bought. But swapping is still a wonderful way to save money.

What do you have that I could use? What do I have that you need? Perhaps one of the most obvious things to swap is children's clothing. Most clothing can be worn by several children, especially by two- or three-year-olds, who grow too fast to wear it out.

Children's clothing, children's furniture, children's toys are all well made, and the need for them quickly passes. This is a good place to swap with other families.

Some churches set up places where swapping can take place. Instead of having a garage sale, why not have a neighborhood swap meet, where goods are exchanged, not money?

Swap housework, swap expertise, swap bedding plants. Swap houseplant cuttings, swap days driving the kids to school, swap baby-sitting.

Swapping can be arranged informally (talking with a neighbor over the back fence) or formally (putting an ad in the paper). There is, in most papers, a column for just this. This column is fun to read. I've never found anything I wanted to swap, but I might someday.

What Are the Neighbors Throwing Out?

Don't laugh, and don't cringe. People throw away tons of good items every year. Most of them feel guilty about what they are throwing away and would be relieved if someone would take it off their hands.

It seems that people who live in apartment complexes are especially quick to throw away useful and often new items. I suppose this is because they move often and are constantly unburdening themselves of extra possessions.

Back of the apartment complex where I am living there is a huge open area of fields and hills. I find all kinds of things there—chicken wire, scraps of wood, used bricks. Someone threw a sofa bed up on the hill. Every time I walk by it, I try to think of someone who could use a good sofa frame. To use it, one would have to strip off all the upholstery, right down to the frame, then have the whole thing rebuilt. I can't think of anyone who needs it, so it just sits.

It might cost more to redo the sofabed than to buy a new one, but what a waste to leave a piece of furniture rotting. People throw good things away because it's easier than finding someone to give them to. Keep your eyes open for items you can use that your neighbors are tossing out. Anything you get for free, you don't have to buy.

Free Animals

We have a problem with overpopulation of domestic pets in this country. Thousands and thousands of animals are put to death every day because their owners did not take the necessary measures to prevent their pets from producing unwanted babies. Spaying and neutering of animals is a simple way to eliminate this problem.

Another problem is that of careless overbreeding in puppy mills. These puppy mills produce puppies for resale in shops around the country. The conditions the breeding animals live in are atrocious. Their only function is to breed one litter after another so their owners can sell the pups and make a living.

Often the puppies are sick, or have hidden genetic problems that surface later, after you've taken them home and begun to love them. It's very sad for a family that has such an animal.

Pure-bred pets cost a lot of money, and it's an investment you know you'll eventually lose. Your family has to decide if you want to make the investment in an expensive animal. There could be another way.

Almost every day the newspaper carries ads offering animals for free. I have seen ads for almost every kind of purebred dog imaginable, because an owner was moving somewhere the pet would not be welcome.

Before investing in an expensive puppy from a store in a mall, see if you can find one for free. Or check the local humane society. The only fees there are for shots and spaying or neutering. In some cases there are no fees at all, just a suggested contribution.

If you tell the humane society people what you are looking for and are patient, you will probably get what you want eventually. Our beautiful blonde cocker spaniel came from the pound. She had just been groomed and was as pretty as any dog you've ever seen. She's been a great pet.

I'm sure you know that kittens are easy to adopt without a dime. I'm sure you've been at the supermarket and seen someone with a box of kittens or puppies and a sign that says "Free."

It's also possible to obtain rabbits, birds, and many other species without spending a dollar. In fact, if you have the space, it is possible to get wild mustangs several places in the country. These wild horses are overpopulating and threatening range land. The government periodically rounds them up and offers them to whomever can care for them.

I just heard a story that tore at my heart. It seems that when greyhounds used for racing have lost their speed, they are killed. There is a movement afoot to find homes for these wonderful, gentle animals, rather than seeing them exterminated.

So before you rush off to a pet store, think about some other alternatives for obtaining a pet. It costs plenty after you get the animal, to care for it and have it licensed. If you can get an animal that is right for your family for free, you have saved a lot of money.

The Public Library

Perhaps one of the great treasure houses of free services is the public library. I am continually amazed at what libraries today offer, in addition to books.

169

If you haven't been to a library lately, go this week. Not only do libraries offer books, but records, CDs, cassettes, videos, magazines, artwork, pamphlets on every subject you can think of, free information, and free services.

Years ago, when our children were small and we had very little money, I discovered that you can check out an art print from the library and have it in your home for a number of weeks. I had a couple of places in the house where there was a wall hook for hanging framed prints from the library. We had some unusual prints over the years. Some of them were rather extreme and nothing I would have spent money on, but because they were free and the purpose was education, I put them up and we talked about them. See what your library offers in the way of artwork.

The local library is also a great source of information about many subjects. In one town, the library conducted master gardener sessions. A master gardener would come in about once a month and answer questions on gardening.

Other programs focused on taxes, crime prevention, decorative arts, pet care, and a lot more. A great attempt is being made in many cities to make the library a user-friendly place.

Another source of information in many libraries is an information line. You can call and ask the most obtuse question and usually get an answer.

When writing my last book, I had put a quote in the book that I picked up from some secondary source. The publisher questioned the exact source of the quote, and it was my task to find out where it had come from. I called the library information line and asked them. Within a half-hour, I had my answer and more information than I could possibly use. All I did was pick up the phone and call.

I have also found, when researching a topic, that most librarians love to get involved. They find sources and books that I never thought of, and they act as if it is the most important thing they have to do that day.

I visited our local library just to see what free services are available. Once more, I was amazed. While the library seemed to be quite busy, I still wondered how many people even begin to understand what a treasure house of information it is.

First of all, there's tax information. All of the needed tax forms are available from a well-stocked rack. There are recommended books on taxes available for checkout. There is an information sheet that tells when local tax offices are open and where they are located. There is a listing of toll-free numbers for patrons to call for help with taxes. There is a volunteer income-tax assistance program held right in the library facilities; the information piece gives the location and times. And to go the extra mile, the library remains open until midnight on April 15. That evening there is a representative from the U.S. Postal Service available at a drive-up window to collect the completed tax forms. There is a representative from the state revenue office who answers questions, volunteers are available in force, and there is even a stamp machine with a bill changer available. How's that for service?

Another wonderful feature the local library offers is database information. You pay a two dollar surcharge and eleven dollars per hour online. A trained library searcher can recommend the databases that are most appropriate for the information you need. The library also provides lists of databases available in your area.

To keep costs to a minimum, the library staff searcher can perform an initial online search that results in a printout of bibliographic references. These can be used to get the full text of a document from the library.

You can tell the searcher how much you can afford, and he or she will help you get the most information possible for the least amount of money.

Our local library also has a database called Maggie's Place. When you log onto this database, this is the kind of information available:

1. Public access catalog—a listing of all the library district's book, video, audio, and CD collections.
2. A collection of databases—social and community agencies, community calendar, child-care sources, clubs, edu-

171

cation opportunities, local authors, senior housing options, arts, and much more.

3. Encyclopedia and other references.
4. Local government databases that provide information about all local and civic activities.
5. Menus of other library systems.

The library also sponsors a Great Books Discussion Group of adults interested in reading and discussing great literary works. The groups have from ten to twenty people in them. The choice of material for discussion is classical literature such as *The Federalist* by Hamilton, Jay, and Madison, and *The City of God* by Saint Augustine. It is free except for the materials, which you must purchase and read.

The library system also has an extensive bookmobile system, making it possible to check out books at twenty different locations throughout the city.

Children's Services seeks to provide stimulation and learning for children through the sixth grade. There are story times, summer reading programs, and a spring and winter film festival.

There is one more free program worthy of mention, and that is the Right to Read program, which teaches adults how to read on a one-to-one basis. Volunteer tutors are trained, then matched to a compatible student.

A newsletter and calendar page highlight all these events and help you keep them straight. All this for free!

Free Sporting Events

In talking about this chapter with some ladies in a computer repair store, I learned some interesting information. (That's often how you learn the best tips.) I was telling them about the free concerts at the Air Force Academy. They told me that the academy also offers free sporting events from time to time and that boxing events were coming up soon.

That started me thinking about other free sporting events that a family could enjoy together. Here in Colorado Springs, of course, Olympic ice skaters train at the ice rink at the world-famous Broadmoor Hotel. I've found that you can walk in and watch them practice. Of course, it is not a performance, and they do the same routines over and over again, but it gives you a different perspective on the fluid, artistic performances seen on television.

Most families are all too aware of the free opportunities their children have for participation in all kinds of team sports. There is Little League baseball, football, field hockey, and in some places the strangest sport of all—rugby. (I've watched rugby games and never could figure out what the purpose was supposed to be, unless you count seeing how dirty you can get.)

There are plenty of participatory sports activities for children that are free. But what about those professional games that are so expensive? Most professional teams offer free tickets to organizations, and there are even free days. Get a schedule from a team near you or in a city you might be visiting, and find out what they are offering and when.

Your Turn

I have only begun to suggest the places and ways you can get things free. A friend told me that her family used to look behind flower shops on Saturday evenings because the florists threw out flowers that were still good but wouldn't last the weekend.

I looked in the local paper and found an entire column that's not quite free, but you don't need any money to shop. It's called the "Maverick" column, and it lists trades. You can trade anything from a storm door to a kennel for transporting a large dog. Many of the ads suggest an exchange "for something of equal value." That's almost as good as free.

I also sent for a newsletter put out by some very thrifty people in New England. It's called *The Tightwad Gazette*. Each issue has dozens of ideas for saving money. The sample copy I received also had some tips for "getting it free." The authors suggested that when you need something, you let it be known what you want. Be ready to pay a fair price for the item, but

173

often if someone has the item in storage, the owner may just decide to give it to you.

If you're interested in seeing a free copy of the *Tightwad Gazette,* send a self-addressed, stamped envelope to: *Tightwad Gazette,* RR1, Box 3570, Leeds, ME 04263-9710.

I think I've given you enough tips to get you started. It's your turn now. Go see what you can find "for free." If you'll excuse me, I think I'll go plant some of the houseplant cuttings I've exchanged with friends, and then I'll work on the birdhouse I'm making from those scraps of wood I picked up in the field the other day—all for free!

Family Adventures for Little or No Money

- Build a dam across a small stream. Splash around in the pool formed behind the dam. When you are finished, return everything to its natural state.
- Play an old-fashioned game with your kids like Kick the Can or Hide and Seek. They'll love it.
- Mix up a batch of salt dough and keep it in the refrigerator for impromptu projects.
- Get an outdated wallpaper book. Let the kids make their own greeting cards or book covers.
- Cut pictures from old greeting cards to use as decorations or name tags on packages or to make new greeting cards.

11

GET IT CHEAP

ecently I took inventory of the furniture I have and the furniture I need to make life more comfortable. I am a reader, and I tend to stack and stash books all around. I may be reading three or four books at one time. I began to think how nice it would be to have a great big coffee table in the family room as a place to put some of the books I'm reading.

I've never had a family room coffee table. It always seemed that it would be in the line of traffic and just be something to bump my shins against. But in anticipation of a new house and a new floor plan, it seemed a good idea.

I love the country look and old things, so I haunt flea markets, antique shops, thrift stores, garage sales, estate sales, and anywhere else I think I might find a bargain.

In a thrift shop, I spotted a big square, antique oak table with huge, bulbous carved legs. I checked the price and decided it cost more than I wanted to pay. Besides, I wasn't quite ready for it, so I went away and tried to forget it. Then I learned that the thrift shop marks items down after thirty days, so I went back and checked the date. I found it would be reduced in two days.

Two days later I went back. I was sure someone else would have purchased it, but guess what? It was still there, and I asked the clerk how much it would be reduced. "Twenty-five percent," she said. I pulled the table out (the legs had been removed) to give it a better inspection. I found staples all around the edge on the underside of the top. Someone had covered the top with fake leather, and it had been pulled off, leaving the staples. As a result, the tabletop had been protected from damage. The legs had suffered some damage, but I would need to cut them down, anyway, and that would eliminate the damaged area.

Needless to say, I am quite happy with my purchase. I do have quite a little work to do on it, but it will be worth the effort.

Now I'm watching a lovely hand-blown glass piece that will be marked down next week. If I don't get it, that's fine, but if I do, it will be for a fraction of the already inexpensive price. In other words, I thought I had a good thing going when I started finding things in thrift shops. Now I find out that, if I'm patient, I can get them for even less. You, too, can get it, whatever "it" is, for less, if you are patient.

Salvage Shops

Every area has a salvage shop where building materials are recycled. Depending on your needs and expertise, these are wonderful places to shop for bargains. It is possible to buy exquisite old tiles, turned bric-a-brac from Victorian houses, paneling that has been stripped from the interior of old buildings, used brick, light fixtures, plumbing and fixtures, and everything else that can be removed from a building.

These places are usually cold, drafty, and very dirty, but if you need something cheap for a building project, you'll find it here.

If you establish a relationship with the owner of the place and let him know what it is you are looking for, he will probably keep an eye open for what you need. Right now I'm looking for some hand-painted Delft tile for a fireplace. I'm not sure where

I'm going to find them, but I stop by the building salvage place once in a while and walk around, looking at what's there.

There are other kinds of salvage stores. The most common of these are the army and navy surplus stores. I'm not sure anything there ever came anywhere near the army or navy, but that's what they are called, and they're fun to visit.

Recently I needed a piece of foam padding to use for a sleeping pad. I was looking for some in a fabric store and overheard two gentlemen discussing the price. One of them said, "The only place to buy foam padding is at the surplus store."

"Excuse me," I said. "Could you tell me how to get there? I was ready to buy this, but if I can get it for less and the surplus store is not too far away, I'll go there."

They told me where it is, and I went. I was amazed at the variety of things in the store. Much of it wasn't worth looking at, but such things as outerwear, all-weather gear, wool socks, caps, mittens and gloves, camping supplies, and garden tools were real bargains. The foam was there, and it was about one-third less in price.

There are also stores that sell damaged goods. There is a considerable amount of freight damage to goods moved across the country. It can be cases of canned foods that are perfectly safe, but for some reason cannot be sold in regular stores. It can be a piece of furniture that may have a tiny bit of damage (or a lot—check it out).

Office supplies seem to accumulate in salvage stores. You can buy anything you would use in an office and at a fraction of the price.

Greeting cards, wrapping paper, labels, and ribbons can usually be found in salvage shops. I once bought a bolt of shiny blue ribbon for wrapping gifts. I am still using it after several years. The bolt was about a foot across, and I paid only a couple of dollars for it.

Other items to look for in this kind of shop are packaged food items, shoes, boots, decorative items for your home, small appliances, clothing, toys, and sometimes even drugstore items like vitamins.

Some people are intimidated by the jumble of things in a salvage store. It helps if you go with something definite in mind. Ask the clerks where you might find such an item. Believe it or not, they have a pretty good idea where everything is. If you have the time, you might see a trip to such a store as a recreational adventure for your family on a rainy afternoon.

Swap Meets

For some people, swap meets may be going too far in the money-saving business. Swap meets are usually held in a field or near an auction barn on a Saturday or Sunday. Those with goods to sell rent a space, back their vehicles (of all kinds and conditions) into a space, open the trunk, and spread out their goods, sometimes on tables and sometimes on the ground.

Buyers walk up and down the rows, looking at all this stuff, from cheap plastic toys to old pieces of furniture. You can buy fabric, baseball cards, old and new tools, rugs, handcrafts, old and new china—truly almost anything you can think of.

Recently, for fun, I went to a swap meet on a Saturday afternoon. The one thing I found that interested me (but not enough to buy it) was a serger for sewing. It was at a very reasonable price and looked in great condition. I asked the seller about the equipment. He said he had purchased it from a store that had gone bankrupt. It was brand new.

What's swapped most at swap meets is conversation. People stand around talking to each other, and they are willing to talk with you. It is a lot of fun.

There are people who follow the swap-meet circuit and make a living selling at them. Watch these people pack and unpack. They have it down to a science. Then there are people from your community who have cleaned out their garage and want to sell the excess. Swap meets are like a gigantic garage sale.

Perhaps the most interesting swap meet I've ever been to is held in Shipshawana, Indiana. This is in the heart of the Amish country, and the Amish people bring their wonderful handcrafted items to sell. It is possible to buy handmade quilts, lace, knit goods, handcrafted furniture, and unbelievably delicious food products. There is an air of stepping back a century to a simpler time, when the county fair was the biggest event of the year.

Garage Sales

Garage sales are fun to have and to attend. They're a good way to rid yourself of excess stuff, if you don't mind setting up and running the sale.

I know a couple that has traveled to Europe several times in the last few years. They've acquired the funds to travel by buying pieces of furniture at garage sales, fixing them up, and reselling them at their own garage sale.

Once when they were visiting, we made the rounds of garage sales. One of the things my friend bought was a golf-club bag that had several clubs in it but not a complete set. At home he had several other clubs and he planned to build a complete set, which he would then sell for a good price. Because I was out with them, I ended up buying a brand-new four-man rubber raft for seventeen dollars.

Another time I went to a garage sale with my brother. He bought a Stanley wood plane for twenty-five cents. It had been laying in the corner of someone's garage for a number of years and was very dirty and rusty. Within fifteen minutes of getting it home, he had it cleaned up like new. Since his hobby is restoring wooden boats, he was delighted to have another plane.

Perhaps the delight of thrift shopping is the serendipity of it all. You just never know what you will find next. Often the item you find may not be of great value, unless you need it and get it for much less than you would pay at a department store, in which case it has great value to you. You can save money on that item and use the money you save for a family outing.

As has been so aptly said, "One man's trash is another man's treasure." If you don't believe that statement, have your own garage sale and put a price on the stuff you are sure no one would ever want. Watch what happens. My experience in garage sales is limited, because I would rather give things away than set up and tend a garage sale. But once I did have a sale, and I put together several boxes of items that I truly thought belonged in the trash can. A friend said, "Try to sell it. You can always throw it away later. I think you'll be surprised what they'll buy." I think I put a price of one dollar on each box. Those boxes were among the first to go.

Although you can buy anything at a garage sale, some of the best buys are in furniture, appliances, children's clothing, sporting equipment and games, collector's items such as baseball cards and china, camping gear, and automotive products such as tires and carrying racks.

Clothing for adults is usually dated or worn, and household linens are usually nearly worn out. Unless you are buying these items for rags or knock-about clothing, they aren't good buys.

Auctions and Everything Else

I have little experience with auctions. It is one of the areas I'd like to learn more about in the next year. There is a local auction here in the city every Monday evening, and I know it is possible to inspect the items for auction on Saturdays.

The items sold at auction can sometimes, although not always, be of a higher quality than those found at other sources. It is important to inspect the items of interest. Our local paper always carries a listing of the items that will be on the auction block. If something sounds right for your needs, go inspect it before the bidding begins.

Set a limit to how much you will spend on the item, and then stick to it. In the frenzy of acquisition, it is easy to get carried away.

Watch the newspapers for unusual sales such as ones the U.S. Post Office, the local police department, and the Customs Offices hold for seized or abandoned goods. There are some phenomenal bargains to be found here.

Conclusion

I believe there is a way to beat the high cost of living. I believe it takes some concentration, some attention to what's available, some effort to find those hidden bargains. I think for some people, it takes a change of mind-set. The local thrift shop is not Saks or Nordstroms.

What I like to do is save all the money I can on everything possible, so that once in a while I can go to a department store and buy something I've wanted for a long time. I visit these stores with regularity, whether I buy or not. It is a wonderful way of improving my taste, of staying knowledgeable about what is available, and of being able to recognize brand names and the most up-to-date styles when I find them other places.

Another inexpensive way of keeping abreast of changing styles, changing trends in home decorating, changing ideas, and changing automobile design and development is to read magazines. I usually pick up a *Vogue* pattern magazine as soon as it hits the newsstand. *Vogue* styles run almost two years ahead of retail stores, so I can know what's coming into fashion far before it hits the stores.

Popular home magazines give you lots of ideas and tips for decorating and fixing up your home. Many magazines tell you how to do it yourself and save money. Remember the table I told you I bought for a coffee table? Well, the legs are detached, and I'm not sure how they should be put back. A current magazine tells how to reattach legs to an old table. How timely!

There are two ways, at least, to approach this whole business of saving money when you shop. One is to feel sorry for yourself that you don't have enough money to go to the finest stores and shop. The other—the one I recommend—is to see it all as a great adventure. You never know what you'll find next; you never know what truly great treasure you might find. You can enjoy the purchase because it didn't cost an arm and a leg. You can use it because you don't have your life savings tied up in that one item. You can get rid of it when you're finished with it for the same reason. And once in a while, you can take your family someplace truly special, without financial stress and without guilt, because you've been thrifty with your money and you've saved for this event.

The release of guilt associated with spending too much money on a vacation can of itself be restorative. Some family vacations are nothing but times of stress, and one reason why can be the amount of money the family is spending.

If you learn to spend wisely throughout the year, you will have the necessary funds to enjoy day-to-day family fun, yearly vacations, and a sane, fiscally sound life.

Family Adventures for Little or No Money

- Make a calendar for Grandma and Grandpa by drawing twelve pictures and gluing them on another calendar. Or on a copy machine, run twelve pages with a grid at the bottom for the dates and blank at the top for the children's pictures. Help the kids fill in the dates.

- Form a rhythm band using pot lids and wooden spoons, wax paper fastened around combs (the children can hum to make an interesting sound), and/or milk jugs filled with dried beans. Put on some lively music and let the children play.

- Have the kids see how many different varieties of a certain thing they can find (like leaves, rocks, flowers, bugs, buttons).

- Let your children put on a play—perhaps you can write your own. Help them collect costume materials and decide where to perform.

- Get a big box from an appliance store and give it to the kids. Watch their imaginations take over.

- Begin a family history by interviewing family members. Using a cassette recorder, have them tell stories. Sometimes it helps older family members who might be intimidated by a tape recorder to be interviewed with a group. As one begins to talk, others add their viewpoints to the story. These tapes will be treasured in years to come when family members have died.

ENDNOTES

Chapter 1

1. Larry Burkett, *Family Budgets That Work*, Pocket Guides (Wheaton, Ill.: Tyndale House Publishers, 1988), p. 14.
2. Gwen Weising, *Raising Kids on Purpose for the Fun of It* (Tarrytown, N.Y.: Fleming H. Revell, 1989).
3. Larry Burkett, *Using Your Money Wisely* (Chicago, Ill.: Moody Press, 1985), p. 18.

Chapter 2

1. Ron and Judy Blue, *Money Matters* (Nashville, Tenn.: Thomas Nelson, 1988), p. 55.
2. Claudia Wallis, "Onward, Women!" *Time* (December 4, 1989), p. 82.
3. Ibid.
4. Sandra Schocket, *Summer Jobs: Finding Them, Getting Them, Enjoying Them* (Princeton, N.J.: Peterson's Guides, 1985).
5. Charlene Canape, *The Part-time Solution* (New York: Harper and Row, 1990) p. 2.
6. Marsha Sinetar, *Do What You Love, the Money Will Follow* (New York: Dell Publishing, 1987), p. 7.

Chapter 3

1. Mary Rowland, "Parents Must Teach Children about Financial Responsibility," *New York Times* (1991).
2. Lilian G. Katz and Sylvia C. Chard, *Engaging Children's Minds: The Project Approach* (Norwood, N.J.: Ablex Publishing, 1989).
3. Rowland, *New York Times.*

4. Sylvia Porter, *Sylvia Porter's New Money Book for the 80's* (New York: Doubleday, 1979), pp. 31–33.

5. Larry Burkett, *The Complete Financial Guide for Young Couples* (Wheaton, Ill.: Victor Books, 1989), pp. 159–60.

6. Ibid., pp. 159–72.

7. Donald Hall, "We Are Stingy on a Soul-Level Far Deeper Than the Tax-Level," *Yankee* (September 1991), p. 58.

Chapter 7

1. Edith Schaeffer, *Hidden Art* (Wheaton, Ill.: Tyndale House, 1971), p. 66.

2. Gwen Weising, *Finding Time for Family Fun* (Tarrytown, N.J.: Fleming H. Revell Co., 1991), pp. 127–28.

Chapter 8

1. Ron Blue, *A Woman's Guide to Financial Peace of Mind* (Colorado Springs, Colo.: Focus on the Family, 1991), p. 62.

2. Ibid.

3. Ibid.

4. Sylvia Porter, *Sylvia Porter's New Money Book for the 80's* (New York: Doubleday, 1979), p. 347.

5. Blue, *Woman's Guide,* p. 63.

‘BIBLIOGRAPHY

How to Manage Your Money

Blue, Ron. *Master Your Money.* Nashville, Tenn.: Thomas Nelson, 1991.

———. *A Woman's Guide to Financial Peace of Mind.* Colorado Springs, Colo.: Focus on the Family, 1991.

Blue, Ron and Judy. *Money Matters.* Nashville, Tenn.: Thomas Nelson, 1988.

Burkett, Larry. *The Complete Financial Guide for Young Couples.* Wheaton, Ill.: Victor Books, 1989.

———. *Family Budgets That Work.* Wheaton, Ill.: Tyndale House Pocket Books, 1977.

———. *Using Your Money Wisely.* Chicago: Moody Press, 1985.

Porter, Sylvia. *Sylvia Porter's New Money Book for the 80's.* New York: Doubleday, 1979.

Rushford, Patricia H. *Lost in the Money Maze.* Lynnwood, Wash.: Aglow Publications, 1991.

Thoene, William Brock. *Protecting Your Income and Your Family's Future.* Minneapolis, Minn.: Bethany House, 1989.

Van Caspel, Venita. *The Power of Money Dynamics.* Reston, Va.: Reston Publishing, 1983.

Ideas for Inexpensive Family Fun

Arp, Claudia. *Beating the Winter Blues.* Nashville, Tenn.: Thomas Nelson, 1991.

———. *Sanity in the Summertime.* Nashville, Tenn.: Thomas Nelson, 1991.

Cooley, Vivian. *Time for Snails and Painting Whales.* Chicago: Moody Press, 1987.

Dow, Emily R. *Now What Shall We Do?* New York: M. Barrows and Co., Inc., 1966.

Nagle, Avery, and Joseph Leeming. *Kitchen Table Fun.* Philadelphia: J. B. Lippincott Co., 1961.

Peel, Kathy, and Joy Mahaffey. *A Mother's Manual for Holiday Survival.* Colorado Springs, Colo.: Focus on the Family Publishing, 1991.

———. *A Mother's Manual for Schoolday Survival.* Colorado Springs, Colo.: Focus on the Family Publishing, 1990.

———. *A Mother's Manual for Summer Survival.* Colorado Springs, Colo.: Focus on the Family Publishing, 1989.

General Books on the Family

Birkey, Verna, and Jeanette Turnquist. *Building Happy Memories and Family Traditions.* Old Tappan, N.J.: Fleming H. Revell Co., 1980.

Chapman, Steve and Annie, with Maureen Bank. *Gifts Your Kids Can't Break.* Minneapolis, Minn.: Bethany House, 1991.

Pride, Mary. *All the Way Home.* Westchester, Ill.: Crossway Books, 1989.

Schaeffer, Edith. *Hidden Art.* Wheaton, Ill.: Tyndale House, 1971.

———. *What Is a Family?* Old Tappan, N.J.: Fleming H. Revell Co., 1975.

Weising, Gwen. *Finding Time for Family Fun.* Tarrytown, N.Y.: Fleming H. Revell Co., 1991.

———. *Raising Kids on Purpose for the Fun of It.* Tarrytown, N.Y.: Fleming H. Revell Co., 1989.